Sober Living
WORKBOOK

Sober Living
WORKBOOK
Rip O'Keefe, Ph.D.

First Published, August, 1980

ISBN: 0-89486-093-3

Printed in the United States of America

Editor's Note:
  Hazelden Educational Materials offers a variety of information on chemical dependency and related areas. Our publications do not necessarily represent Hazelden or its programs, nor do they officially speak for any Twelve Step organization.

TABLE OF CONTENTS

Week Four

Acknowledgments

First and foremost I must acknowledge the many suffering alcoholics who allowed me to share in their illness and recovery from alcoholism. Of course my indebtedness to my many friends in Alcoholics Anonymous for teaching me the strength, beauty and success of the Twelve Steps of A.A. must be recognized. Many colleagues have helped to shape my thinking and development of this treatment manual, most important of whom is a colleague, friend and wife, Dr. Beth Egan O'Keefe. I cannot omit the many valuable discussions and suggestions made by Sam Moreno, M.Ed., Dr. Thomas Tourlentes, and Don and Linda Vermeire both of whom are certified alcoholism counselors. Finally, I cannot forget the three typists who have transformed my scribble and scrawl into legible manuscript, Mrs. Kim VonMotz, Mrs. Darla Hartzler and Mrs. Tamara Purcell.

ROK

Introduction

The *Sober Living Workbook* is designed to assist alcoholics* in their recovery from alcoholism. The workbook is a tool to be used by the recovering alcoholic while in treatment as an outpatient or an inpatient, or by persons in an aftercare program, or by men and women who have been sober some time and who now desire a "refresher course." The workbook helps the individual to achieve or to improve upon a state we call "sober living."

For an alcoholic, sober living is abstinence from alcoholic beverages and healthy adjustment of thoughts and feelings. Sober living is a life-style of growth and accomplishment. Sober living is a zest for each day, a total commitment to a happy and productive life.

There are three essential underpinnings or philosophical beliefs behind this workbook. They are: 1) Recovery from alcoholism means continuous abstinence from alcoholic beverages; 2) Abstinence is the avoidance of alcohol; and 3) Recovery comes through following the Twelve Steps of Alcoholics Anonymous. The Twelve Steps are:

1. "We admitted we were powerless over alcohol—that our lives had become unmanageable."
2. "Came to believe that a Power greater than ourselves could restore us to sanity."
3. "Made a decision to turn our will and our lives over to the care of God *as we understood Him.*"
4. "Made a searching and fearless moral inventory of ourselves."
5. "Admitted to God, to ourselves, and to another human being the exact nature of our wrongs."
6. "Were entirely ready to have God remove all these defects of character."

---

*When the words "alcohol, alcoholic, drinking and sobriety" are used in this workbook, they can be substituted with "chemicals, chemically dependent, using and chemically free." The workbook is useful for both the chemically dependent person and the alcoholic.

7. "Humbly asked Him to remove our shortcomings."
8. "Made a list of all persons we had harmed, and became willing to make amends to them all."
9. "Made direct amends to such people wherever possible, except when to do so would injure them or others."
10. "Continued to take personal inventory and when we were wrong promptly admitted it."
11. "Sought through prayer and meditation to improve our conscious contact with God *as we understood Him*, praying only for knowledge of His will for us and the power to carry that out."
12. "Having had a spiritual awakening as the result of these steps, we tried to carry this message to alcoholics, and to practice these principles in all our affairs."*

Sober living is well-balanced living. Well-balanced living is the orderly arrangement of significant parts of life. It is the ability to do all that we *have* to do in an appropriate fashion, and still have time for many of the healthy, enjoyable things we *want* to do.

Well-balanced living recognizes the need for regular biological rhythms such as routinely getting to bed at about the same time, getting up on time, eating well-balanced meals each day and exercising regularly. Well-balanced living also deals with our psychological needs by making our thinking clear and effective, generating appropriate and healthy emotions, and solving daily problems in a productive and positive manner. Well-balanced living recognizes sociological needs such as taking care of interpersonal demands from family and friends, practicing responsible citizenship and being a giver to the world rather than being only a taker. Finally, but equally important, well-balanced living recognizes our spiritual needs such as having a truly "spiritual" faith, practicing this faith, and living a life consistent with our spiritual beliefs.

*The Twelve Steps reprinted with permission of A.A. World Services, Inc.

The *Sober Living Workbook* takes a day-to-day approach which practically and functionally teaches sober living. This workbook is not just a book about alcoholism. It is a *work* book. A book that requires you to work. Sober living is hard work. You cannot wish yourself into sober living. This workbook, in concert with an alcoholism treatment program or in conjunction with A.A. attendance, will help teach you how to achieve the art of sober living.

If you intend to use this book in a treatment program for alcoholism, each day you need to complete all that is required of you; to write, to think or to feel. Recovery from alcoholism requires serious commitment each day, not just while completing the twenty-eight days of the workbook, but for the rest of your life. If you intend to make that commitment, then sober living is yours for the taking.

If you are not in a treatment program, but rather are using this workbook to strengthen your sobriety, you may not be able to do the exercises according to schedule. That is fine. Go through the workbook at your own pace. However, the workbook does have a definite plan of development. Each chapter builds on what has gone before. Even if you do not stick to the suggested daily and weekly schedules, it would be best if you took each chapter in order, rather than jumping ahead or going back and forth through the chapters.

You will need a notebook. Whenever you answer a question, write the answer in your notebook. There is no space for your answer in the workbook. Your notebook will become a record of the twenty-eight days you spend working on sober living. Please get a notebook before you start.

Orientation Day—*Came to believe . . .*

Welcome

Offer yourself congratulations for your decision to seek treatment for your alcoholism or to strengthen your sobriety. Perhaps a word of encouragement and advice is in order to those who are seeking treatment. Many people start alcohol treatment programs. These people seek treatment, we assume, because drinking has impaired some significant part of their lives. Sometimes, they decide to start such a program on their own. More often, pressures from a spouse, a family physician, an employer, a clergyman, or even a judge have much to do with their decision to seek treatment.

Treatment for alcoholism is different from treatment for most other illnesses. The treatment of alcoholism requires that the patient be active rather than passive. It is a mistake for the alcoholic to lie back and say, "Doctor, make me better." Alcoholism is an illness which requires the alcoholic virtually to treat himself. To say this is not to minimize the efforts of others. It is only an attempt to point out that the alcoholic will recover from alcoholism only by changing the way he lives.

How can the alcoholic treat himself or herself? The answer is simple. By a decision never to drink again. Then, daily, for the rest of his or her life to practice sober living.

What? How many times have you said things like, "I'll never drink again," or, "I'll never get drunk again," or "I'll quit for two weeks," or, "I'll only drink one or two," only to find out each time that sooner or later you were back at it? What? You say you've tried determination, promises, prayers, hopes, lies, only to find that sooner or later you returned to drinking?

In other words, you say that deciding to quit drinking is not sufficient for you? Exactly. A decision to quit drinking is easy and is good only until you decide to start drinking again. Your problem is that you only decided to quit drinking; you did not begin to practice sober living. It's as simple as that.

If you decide to quit drinking, and if you then take up the practice of sober living, you will not drink. It is that easy.

Perhaps, we should slow down. This workbook is designed

to make you think, to make you feel, and most importantly, to teach you sober living. Don't be overwhelmed, we'll go slowly. We'll take it one day at a time.

Learning Sober Living

This workbook teaches sober living through the practice of sober living. The workbook relies upon the Twelve Steps of A.A. as the primary road to recovery. It supplements the Twelve Steps of A.A. with activities and exercises that teach well-balanced, healthy living. The workbook includes eight activities for each day, and guides the recovering alcoholic through twenty-eight days.

The importance of the workbook is not only in teaching the Twelve Steps of A.A., but also in teaching their implementation. In the workbook, we focus upon healthy thinking and healthy feeling, put together into an active, sober life. Sober living is thinking, feeling, and doing what keeps us sober.

Rules For Using The Workbook

a) Start when you are sober. If you are in a treatment program, you may begin the orientation day while you are still sobering up, but do not begin the first day of the workbook until you are sober.

b) There are eight activities for each day. Do each activity according to your personal schedule. Make time. Do not let excuses get in your way. You will find most exercises take a few minutes and even the busiest of people can find a few minutes eight times a day.

c) Stick to a schedule. There is a certain rhythm that the workbook tries to initiate in your life. The schedule below is only a sample, you may want to adjust the hours to fit your schedule, but once you adjust the times, stick to them. Whether you are in treatment or not, take time to make your own schedule now. *Write it in your notebook.*

Workbook Exercises	Optional Schedule	Daily Routine
1) Morning Meditation	6:30 a.m.	Upon Rising
2) Thinking About Yourself	8:00 a.m.	Breakfast
3) Emotional Growth	12:00 p.m.	Lunch
4) Sober Life-Style	3:00 p.m.	Coffee Break
5) Action for the Day	6:00 p.m.	Dinner
6) Feelings: Review of the Day	9:00 p.m.	Beverage Break
7) Daily Reading	11:00 p.m.	While getting ready for bed
8) Evening Reflection	11:30 p.m.	When in bed

d) The four requirements below will help to establish a healthy biological rhythm in your life.

1) Eat three meals a day (morning, noon and evening) while completing this workbook. Do not worry about dieting.

2) Take afternoon and evening beverage breaks. Remember, water is an excellent non-fattening beverage.

3) Go to bed and get up at the same time every day for these four weeks. Do not indulge yourself. Establish a definite sleeping and rising pattern.

4) Exercise daily within your medical limit, if only by taking a walk.

e) If you are still awake after your evening reflection, or if you have problems falling asleep, read ahead to the next day in the workbook. This may be a helpful orientation for the next day.

f) *Write all your answers in your notebook.* Be specific, and answer each question fully.

Program Over-View

Morning Meditation (Upon Rising)

1) Upon rising, read the Morning Meditation and spend a few minutes alone (at least ten) thinking about the topic of the day.

2) Morning Meditation requires you to discipline your thinking. Put the book down and think. If your mind wanders, reread the passage and discipline yourself to concentrate. Meditation is work and it requires energy to pay attention to the topic.

3) During Morning Meditation ask yourself questions such as "How does this pertain to me? How can I apply this meditation to my life?"

4) At its best, meditation becomes more than an intellectual exercise on an uplifting topic. Meditation can internalize our feelings. Further, meditation can help us translate thoughts and feelings into action. If, during morning meditation, we have good thoughts that pertain to sober living, we can then make efforts to implement them.

Thinking About Yourself (Breakfast)

1) Before breakfast turn to the section called "Thinking About Yourself." Many recovering alcoholics have a strong desire to understand the how and the why of their alcoholism. Frankly, the how and the why—even if they could be understood—have little to do with sober living. But there is some value in better understanding yourself.

2) Read through the entire section, then eat your breakfast. This interval gives your unconscious mind time to think about yourself.

3) After breakfast, find a place to be alone and answer in writing the questions asked. Be honest, direct and simple in your answers.

4) You may ask why you need to write your answers instead of just thinking about them. The answer is simple. Writing forces you to be specific in your answers. It also encourages

detailed thought about you and your alcoholism. *Write your answers in your notebook.*

Emotional Growth (Lunch)

1) This is an important exercise. You may be uncomfortable with this exercise and want to rush through it, but work diligently on this section even though it may make you feel uncomfortable.

2) Read the entire section before lunch. This will only take a few minutes. After lunch respond to each question in writing, following the instructions and the suggestions that are given.

3) After you have completed the exercise, spend a few moments in thought. Think about how you can apply each day's exercise in "Emotional Growth" to your daily life.

Sober Life-Style (Coffee Break)

1) Each day at this time, concentrate on habits, virtues, or personal characteristics that you may need to add to your life.

2) Sit alone in a quiet place. Have a cup of coffee or cold beverage and maybe a snack. If you are watching your weight, have a carrot stick or something with just a few calories. It is important for a recovering alcoholic to take time out to rest, to think, and to have a refreshing pause.

3) Read all the way through the exercise. Spend a few minutes thinking about it. Now reread it. This time, write out the answer in your notebook and consider how you may apply this section to your life.

Action for the Day (Dinner)

1) Growth in sober thinking and sober feeling is possible only if we put our healthy thoughts and feelings into action. This section is designed to help you do just that. Do those things that will keep you sober.

2) Read this section before dinner. After your dinner, get to work on each activity. You may feel awkward or uncomfortable with some of the activities. That's OK, do them anyway. Doing them may help keep you sober.

3) Going to an A.A. meeting every night is the soundest possible advice. For the recovering alcoholic, there is an old A.A. saying which reads, "Thirty meetings in thirty days." Don't shy away from this advice. Get to an A.A. meeting every day, if you can. If you don't know how to do this yet you will be told in tomorrow's exercise. If there is no A.A. meeting for you to attend, spend half an hour alone reading from the *Big Book*.

4) Each day do the actions assigned for the day. Doing them may help keep you sober.

Feelings: Review of the Day (Beverage Break)

1) Have a glass of warm milk or a cup of hot cocoa; take time for a liquid refreshment break.

2) This exercise is designed to make you aware of your feelings.

3) Place yourself in a quiet isolated place. Be sensitive to your emotions. Let the full impact of the day hit you.

4) Respond to each question honestly in writing.

5) Following the instructions, review your feelings.

Daily Reading (While getting ready for bed)

1) Take time out each day to read. Reading is a good way to acquire information about alcoholism and recovery.

2) Read the daily selection. Stop several times during the reading to ponder its application to your life.

3) Fill out the questions at the end of the reading.

Evening Reflection (When in bed)

1) It is good to review the day each night before falling asleep.

2) Read the evening reflection. Think about the topic for approximately five minutes.

3) Practice mental discipline. Force yourself to think about your day. If you find your mind wandering, reread the evening reflection.

One Last Thought

1) No drinking.
2) Start the workbook tomorrow morning, when you are at least twenty-four hours sober.
3) Don't try to use this workbook by yourself if you are an alcoholic who has been drinking. Drinking alcoholics need the help of a treatment program, regularly-attended A.A. meetings, and a sponsor. DON'T TRY TO GO IT ALONE.
4) Use the workbook according to the rules of the book as well as the suggestions given in the program over-view section.
5) Live the Twelve Steps of A.A. daily and you will live a successful and sober life.

Do not start this day unless you are at least twenty-four hours sober.

Day One—*First Things First . . .*

Morning Meditation (Upon Rising)

Probably, this is a day of mixed feelings for you. More than likely there is a sense of relief in beginning to do something about your alcoholism. It is also probable that there is a sense of apprehension about what the decision to quit drinking means to you. Bolster your courage and practice the advice given in the Bible to Lot and his wife as they left their town: "Don't look back."

During these few moments in meditation, concentrate on your determination to achieve sober living. Think of all the reasons for this decision. Remember, you have decided to choose sober living and this decision took courage and determination. You should feel pride and a new sense of direction in your life.

For the final few moments, be grateful to all those who helped you decide to stop drinking and to seek treatment for your alcoholism.

Thinking About Yourself (Breakfast)

This section is designed to provoke thought and evaluation of your life and your problems.

Did you know you can think your way out of your alcohol problem? That's right. You are in control of your own destiny. Many people are in the habit of looking to other people, situations or events as the cause of their own failures and problems. Similarly, many people are willing to take responsibility for their successes and achievements, but want to blame some external agent for their mistakes and failures.

There was an A.A. old-timer who pointed out that when things go wrong for people they tend to say, "Why me, Lord?" but when things go well for the same individuals, they never say, "Why me, Lord?" His point was that you can either blame your problems on other people and external causes, or you can look inside yourself and find the energy to change and to solve your problems.

An alcoholic is capable of solving his or her own problems and living a relatively happy life. Many alcoholics do not realize that they are hurting themselves and creating many of their own problems. Some alcoholics do have insight into how they are harming themselves but, for some irrational reason, they continue to drink and create additional problems. Alcoholics are not stupid. They are caught in the trap of alcoholism and don't know how to get out. They don't know how to live a sober life.

Sober living starts with a recognition of the problem. Step One of Alcoholics Anonymous recognizes the problem when it says, "We admitted we were powerless over alcohol—that our lives had become unmanageable."

You are an alcoholic, aren't you? Write your answers in your notebook.

What does being an alcoholic mean to you?

How do you know that you are an alcoholic? List five reasons. In other words, how has your drinking harmed your life?

People try to stop drinking for many different reasons. Why did you decide to stop drinking and seek help for your alcoholism?

Did anyone else want you to begin an alcohol treatment program, or did anyone else ever wish that you would stop drinking? Who and why?

Did you ever try to quit drinking, slow down your drinking, or make other attempts to control your drinking? List the times you did this and why you think these attempts to control your drinking failed.

What have you learned from these attempts to control your drinking?

Make a list of people you think would be happy to hear you are beginning an alcohol treatment program. Try to think of five people. Write their names in your notebook. Give the reasons they would be happy.

Is there anyone who would be upset to find out that you have begun an alcohol treatment program? Force yourself to think of some old drinking buddies or bartenders. Write their names and the reason they would be upset.

Why are you beginning treatment? Write your answer in as much detail as necessary. Be specific and honest. Mention any pressures put on you. Identify any crisis that has guided you to this point. Mention the thoughts and feelings that brought you here. Before writing this answer, reread Step One of A.A.—"We admitted we were powerless over alcohol—that our lives had become unmanageable."

Emotional Growth (Lunch)

Recovery from alcoholism requires courage and honesty. You have taken the first plunge and displayed the courage to start treatment. Praise yourself for your courage; many people lack the strength to do what you have done.

Honesty is next. "We admitted we were powerless over alcohol—that our lives had become unmanageable." This is a strong statement. It requires brutal honesty. There are three essential concepts in this statement:

1) We admitted
2) We were powerless over alcohol
3) Our lives had become unmanageable

Study each segment of this First Step of A.A. Understand the words. Think about each section. Describe in your own words how each thought pertains to you and to your life.

Here is the hard part. Let the thought of the First Step of A.A. sink into your emotions. This is not always easy. It is one thing to say that you are alcoholic, and quite another thing to *feel* that you are powerless, to feel that your life has become unmanageable because of your drinking and to admit these feelings to yourself.

Can you *feel* the truth of Step One? Read Step One and feel the emotional impact of this statement, "We admitted we were powerless over alcohol—that our lives had become unmanageable."

How does the truth of Step One feel inside you? Describe the emotional impact of this step. Write it in your notebook.

What is the difference between intellectually accepting the truth of Step One and emotionally feeling the impact of Step One? Describe this difference in your notebook.

Spend time reading, thinking about, and feeling the meaning of Step One until you can intellectually admit and emotionally feel the truth of this Step in your life.

Sober Life-Style (Coffee Break)

Think of how you have been living, especially over the past year. Apparently, there was sufficient discomfort and distress in your life to pressure you to reach out for help. In order to achieve a sober life-style, one must first stop drinking. Next, in order to recover from alcoholism one needs to systematically do those things that add up to a sober life-style.

Identify the aspects of your life with which you are unhappy. Make this list as long as you want.

Now, take each aspect with which you are unhappy and identify two components: a) what role did your alcoholism have in creating this problem and b) how would you like to resolve this situation? Write in your notebook.

Write a short essay in your notebook entitled *My Sober Life-Style*. Now that you are sober, describe how you would like to live your life. Describe your life as a successful sober, mature, responsible adult.

Action for the Day (Dinner)

This section is designed to bring about sober living on a daily basis. Do each action for the day.

I   Call one person on your list of people who would be happy to find out that you have begun an alcohol treatment program. Choose someone who doesn't know that you have done this. In your conversation, explain to that person why you are seeking alcoholism treatment and what you hope to accomplish through treatment.

II   Here is the hard part for today. Attend an A.A. meeting today. Go. Listen. If you feel like talking and the opportunity arises, say what is on your mind. Do you know what an A.A. meeting is? You probably have heard or read about Alcoholics Anonymous. Maybe you've even gone to A.A. meetings in the past. Briefly, A.A. is a fellowship of men and women who meet together in order to help each other stay sober. It's as simple as that. You cannot practice sober living without A.A. At first you may find many reasons why A.A. won't work for you. Each of those reasons is a self-deception—a lie to yourself. Go to an A.A. meeting because you will find men and women at the meeting who practice sober living. These men and women will be willing to help you, and you can use all the help you can get.

Even though the thought of going to an A.A. meeting may make you nervous, do it. Don't cut corners. Some nervousness and anxiety is part of the price you will have to pay for your recovery from alcoholism. Pay it.

III After the A.A. meeting, stick around for a while, if you can. Introduce yourself to someone. Talk to that person about the role of A.A. in his or her life. If you are riding with someone, talk to that person about A.A.

IV   If you are unable to attend an A.A. meeting, that is, if there is no A.A. meeting that night close enough for you to attend, then spend half an hour in quiet thought and reading. Get your copy of the A.A. *Big Book* and read for half an hour. This half-hour of reading is a backup plan for any night during the next four weeks when it is impossible for you to attend an A.A. meeting. Attend an A.A. meeting daily for the next four weeks—thirty days, thirty meetings.

Don't cut corners. If at all possible attend the A.A. meeting. When that is impossible, read from the *Big Book*.

Feelings: Review of the Day (Beverage Break)

This section is designed to help you to get in touch with your feelings and to express and deal with your feelings in a healthy fashion. Be specific and detailed in your answers.

I   How did you feel talking to the person you telephoned? Write your answer in your notebook.

II How did you feel going to an A.A. meeting? Write your answer in as much detail as possible.

III How do you feel now after working on sober living for a day?

Daily Reading (While getting ready for bed)

This section is designed to increase your knowledge and understanding of alcoholism and other related problems.

What is A.A.?

A.A. stands for Alcoholics Anonymous. A.A. is a fellowship of men and women who, by sharing their experiences, help each other to maintain sobriety. A.A. is a happy mixture of ritual and orthodoxy based on the Twelve Steps and Twelve Traditions.

A.A. was founded by two men who met in 1935. Both were alcoholics and had difficulty maintaining sobriety. Their meeting led to the development of small groups of people in Akron, New York, and Cleveland, who in time became the first A.A. members. From these initial groups, a book emerged in 1939 entitled *Alcoholics Anonymous*. The book is referred to by many in A.A. as their "bible." The book talks about alcohol from the alcoholic's point of view. In it the Twelve Steps are set down with information about their application. The second part of the book contains the personal stories of individuals who sobered up by practicing the Twelve Steps.

From a modest beginning, A.A. has grown to be a worldwide organization that brings hope and sobriety to thousands of people each year. The Twelve Steps of A.A. are based on the principles of healthy living and are imbued with a deep spiritual commitment to a Higher Power.

It is the fellowship of A.A. that helps make A.A. so successful in assisting alcoholics. Fellowship between A.A. members is a deep personal concern for the well-being of other alcoholics.

A.A. is a warm, supportive, and reinforcing society. Newcomers to A.A. are sometimes overwhelmed by the mutual support and trust between A.A. members. Some new members are bothered by such trust and openness. If you are attracted to this group spirit and comradery, you are lucky. If you are inclined not to like the atmosphere of such closeness, you have an additional burden in your recovery from alcoholism. Even if your initial contact with A.A. might leave something to be desired, it is likely that through continued attendance and participation, you will eventually be comfortable. Many people have some initial negative reaction to A.A. We encourage those who may initially be turned off to continue attending. Attitudes do change, and the support that A.A. attendance gives to sober living will be well worth the effort.

What happens at an A.A. meeting? Without going into all the details and workings of A.A., it is safe to say that most meetings start with a moment of silence or reading. Usually there is a discussion organized by a group chairman. The meeting lasts about one hour and ordinarily ends with the Lord's Prayer. If this sounds mysterious, it is meant to. A.A. meetings are anonymous. What happens there, what is said there, who is seen there, stays there. If you want to know more about what goes on at an A.A. meeting, you'll have to go to one.

You may think that you can live soberly without A.A. Maybe you can. A few people do. But if you can't, you'll be drunk again. So, if your major purpose in being in treatment for alcoholism is to achieve sober living, then it seems that you must be willing to do everything possible and/or necessary to achieve your goal. If you're not willing to do what has worked for so many other recovering alcoholics, then perhaps you should review your motives and the degree of honesty with which you took your First Step.

A.A. is the single most effective way to stay sober. Nothing else has worked so well. Even if you are hesitant about going to A.A., bolster your courage and do it. Go to the telephone book and look up Alcoholics Anonymous. Call the number and tell the person who answers that you are an alcoholic, you are sober, and you would like to go to your first A.A. meeting. Ask for instructions to get there. If you need a ride, ask someone to pick you up. Go to a meeting.

At your first A.A. meeting, you need only introduce yourself by your first name. If you can, say you're new and feel a little uncomfortable. More than likely somebody will take you under his/her wing. At this meeting listen carefully; you will probably find many people whose lives were more messed up by alcohol than yours. The important thing, however, is that they are staying sober through participation in A.A.

Before you can decide if A.A. is for you, you must first participate in and be part of the fellowship. Just going to meetings and listening is not enough. To do only that would be like putting on your bathing suit and going to the beach. Those are two essential steps for swimming, but you can't go swimming without actually taking the plunge and getting wet. If you go to A.A. only as an outsider looking in, and if you stay on as an observer, you will never experience the fellowship. In order to experience this fellowship, you will have to take the plunge. You can't just sit back and listen; you will have to talk about yourself, and listen to others talk about themselves. It is this mutual exposure of the truth that leads to the development of trust, understanding, and friendship.

You probably have a dozen reasons why you can't do this. However, the bottom line is this: A.A. is the single most effective way of staying sober. If you want to stay sober, then you might as well stack the cards in your favor and go to A.A.

How often should you go to A.A. meetings? It is up to you. Old-timers in A.A. say that a beginner should go to thirty meetings in thirty days. Though this might sound excessive to you, keep in mind that old-timers have what you want. They are sober. Why not do what they say?

One last observation about A.A. You will only get out of A.A. what you put into it. There is no doubt that it works. If it is not working for you it is probably because you are not putting enough into it. Here is a list of actions you can take to

help you understand the A.A. program:
1) Go to an A.A. meeting every day for a month.
2) Go at least two times a week for the next year.
3) Buy yourself the book entitled *Alcoholics Anonymous,* also called the *Big Book.*
4) Read the book. Reread the book.
5) Practice the Twelve Steps of A.A.
6) Get a sponsor.
7) Talk about yourself at an A.A. meeting.
8) Listen at A.A. meetings and see what others are saying which can benefit you.
9) Visit different A.A. meetings, but when you find the one you like best, make it your home group.
10) Help out before and after meetings. Get involved. Clean ashtrays; make coffee; offer to give rides.

A.A. works. It can work for you if you let it. Remember, A.A. is not just words; it is also actions. Put what you learn from A.A. into your life.

Reading Review

In two or three sentences, describe the point of today's reading.

How does today's reading pertain to you? Give at least two examples.

Can you bring into your life something from today's reading? Write down how you can do that.

Evening Reflection (When in bed)

Read Step One of A.A.: "We admitted we were powerless over alcohol—that our lives had become unmanageable."

Meditate again on the importance of this First Step of A.A. in your life.

Feel gratitude that today you are sober. Reflect on the new direction in your life. Feel good that you are doing something about your drinking problem.

Day Two—*Think, Think, Think . . .*

Morning Meditation (Upon Rising)

This is your second day with the workbook. Think about what you have accomplished so far. You've stopped drinking, you've started your recovery, and you've admitted you are powerless over alcohol—that your life had become unmanageable. These are three significant steps toward recovery. This morning, think of individuals who are happy that you are doing something about your drinking. Think about how fortunate you are to have people who are concerned about you. Rise above resentments you may feel toward those concerned individuals who urged you to seek treatment. Think of how fortunate you are that your drinking didn't drive them away.

Feel gratitude toward these people.

Thinking About Yourself (Breakfast)

Alcoholism is a life problem. It is caused by drinking alcohol to the point that it impairs some part of your life. Drinking can affect your physical health, your job, your marriage and family, your peace of mind, and any other part of your life you can think of.

The alcoholic is usually among the first to recognize that drinking has become a problem. Once aware of this, the alcoholic does many things to cover up or hide the drinking. Seldom does the alcoholic want to stop drinking. Usually, a crisis brings things to a head; then the alcoholic seeks treatment.

You have already answered this question during yesterday's learning; let's ask it again. Are you an alcoholic? Why do you think you are an alcoholic? Write in your notebook.

What convinces you that you are an alcoholic? Be specific. List at least ten things. Focus on actions that are incomplete, commitments that were not kept, promises that were broken. Continue to write in your notebook.

Why did you drink? Give as much detail as possible about the thoughts you used to defend your drinking. In your answer also ask yourself if your *reason* for drinking alcoholic beverages was rational or irrational.

Why did you seek treatment? What happened to make you think about quitting?

When did you drink? Be specific. Focus on feelings. Focus on time. What days? What times?

Where did you drink? Be specific with regard to place and companions.

What did you like about drinking?

Emotional Growth (Lunch)

Alcoholic drinking is an attempt to alter reality. Face it, reality is not all it's cracked up to be. Reality sometimes stinks. People are not always what we want them to be. Some problems have no answers. This is not the best of all possible worlds. So what? You have two choices: 1) to deal with reality the way it is, or 2) to alter reality through alcohol.

The idea that people and situations should be different than they are and that alcohol can help is irrational. Worse than that, it is self-destructive. Most alcoholics deny this. Yet they watch their lives deteriorate as they continue to drink excessively and continue to deny that their drinking is self-destructive.

Alcoholism is an irrational idea built upon the assumption that drinking alcoholic beverages can improve the way things are. Has your drinking ever been a reaction to your feelings or to the way things are? Did you ever use drinking to make things better? If so, how? If not, how did your emotions affect your drinking? Write in your notebook.

Now that you are sober, you see how irrational it was to use alcohol to solve problems. How do you explain that there was a time when you believed alcohol could actually solve your problems?

What irrational ideas caused you to drink?

How do you feel about having had irrational ideas? How do you account for this? Was it self-deception? Was it emotional instability? Why did you have irrational ideas?

Learning to recognize flaws in our thinking is an essential part of recovery. Many of the thoughts of the drinking alcoholic are irrational attempts to deny that drinking is the source of the problems. The ability to recognize your faulty thinking requires emotional growth in the area of honesty and humility.

Sober Life-Style (Coffee Break)

Acknowledging Step One of A.A. is the first part of sobriety, but there must also be an *acceptance* of this Step. Admitting we were powerless over alcohol—that our lives had become unmanageable—can be as objective and noncommittal as admitting that two plus two equals four. We cannot proceed with our recovery until true acceptance has set in.

Accepting Step One of A.A. means letting go. It means giving up all those defenses, maneuvers and rationalizations. It is not just a simple recognition of a self-evident truth—that we are alcoholic—it is also an emotional giving in. We must be able to say, "That's right, I'm an alcoholic, I give up, I surrender."

How does admitting you are an alcoholic change your thinking about yourself? Write in your notebook.

Do you have problems accepting change in your thoughts about yourself? If so, what is the problem? If not, how do you accept yourself now, after Step One of A.A.?

It seems that accepting Step One of A.A.—"We admitted we were powerless over alcohol—that our lives had become unmanageable"—would have an indelible impact upon our lives. How do you think acceptance of Step One of A.A. affects your life? Be specific.

Action for the Day (Dinner)

I   Attend an A.A. meeting. During the meeting listen carefully to what others have to say. Keep in mind that each person at the A.A. meeting has something to offer you. It is up to you to speak up. A.A. has something for everyone, even you. Plunge in.

What did you get out of tonight's A.A. meeting? Do *not* be specific. Remember to keep confidential the people you see and the words you hear at A.A. In general though, what did you get out of the meeting? Write in your notebook.

II Make a list of five things you like that you've observed about A.A.

III Try talking to someone today about yourself. Identify the steps you have already taken to deal with your alcoholism. Identify yourself as an alcoholic; admit that you now recognize your alcoholism, and have begun to do something about it. Write down your reactions to sharing with another person the fact that you are an alcoholic doing something about your alcoholism. How did you feel?

Do you feel that admitting you are an alcoholic and not feeling uncomfortable discussing your disease will eventually help you to stay sober? If so, how? If not, why not?

Feelings: Review of the Day (Beverage Break)

I Many individuals recovering from alcoholism feel depressed and anxious. There is a sense of loss; loss of something desirable like a friend. All too often, the recovering alcoholic fears life without alcohol. A lot of mental energy is wasted thinking about not drinking next week, next month, or even next year.

Review your priorities since you stopped drinking. You have sought treatment for your alcoholism and you have accepted Step One of A.A. Don't feel trapped or hemmed-in; feel a sense of freedom. The monkey is off your back. Find a quiet place and picture yourself free. Feel good. You have broken free. Spend a few minutes alone feeling free from alcohol.

II Drinking has been the "ace in the hole" for most alcoholics prior to their decision to quit. The alcoholic's thinking went something like this: "If things get too tough . . . If I get depressed . . . If I'm nervous . . . If I'm happy . . . If . . ." No matter what happens, you can alter the situation by drinking. If you're down, you can get farther down. If you're up, you can fly. The "ace in the hole" will let you change your feelings.

If you find yourself anxious about the thought of life without alcohol, then don't think about it that way. Take the twenty-four hour approach. The twenty-four hour approach is simply a daily statement that, "I am not going to drink today. I won't worry about tomorrow. I just know I won't drink today." All you have to do is to focus upon today. Do you think this approach can be valuable to you? If not, why not?

III How do you feel about yourself now that you are at the end of your second day of treatment?

Daily Reading (While getting ready for bed)

How Do You Know If You're An Alcoholic?

Old-timers in Alcoholics Anonymous say that the alcoholic is the first to realize the drinking problem, but the last to do something about it. When you're an alcoholic you know it. You are aware that your drinking is harmful to yourself and to others. You know that you drink differently from social drinkers. You know all of this.

The problem is honesty. Most alcoholics who "don't know" if they are alcoholic "don't know" because they don't want to know. They lie to themselves. But deep down inside they know. They know their drinking is different. Even when they say they are telling the total truth, they know they are minimizing, denying, or rationalizing. They only know they do not want to give up drinking. This is what they know best.

Look at it this way. If you agree that alcoholism is a major problem with all kinds of physical, social, psychological, and spiritual side-effects, why not just say to yourself, "Oh well, I don't think that I am an alcoholic, but to avoid that catastrophe, I'll give up drinking." Of course you don't say that because you don't want to quit. You know your drinking is harmful, but you don't want to stop.

Most people who abuse alcohol but don't want to call it "alcoholism" use excuses and denial to protect their drinking. They are afraid to stop drinking. Most people who don't want to stop drinking, although they know their drinking is abnormal, are afraid of life without alcohol. They deny that alcoholism is their problem in order to go on drinking. Once they openly recognize they are alcoholic, they can no longer maintain that their drinking is normal.

Most people who are alcoholic, but who "don't know" that they are alcoholic, take the easy way out. The easy way out, after all, is just that—the easy way out of successful sober living. The easy way out is to say, "I'm not an alcoholic. My drinking is not impairing my life." This self-deceit is the irrational idea that it is easier to avoid facing life's difficulties by drinking than it is to undertake the more rewarding form of life called sober living.

In order to find out if you are an alcoholic, you need to examine all of your responsibilities and commitments to yourself and to others, and then determine whether you are meeting all these obligations. This self-analysis will prove what you know already.

How do you know if you're an alcoholic? You know. You know by your actions, by your thoughts, and by your feelings about your drinking.

What you do when you know you're an alcoholic is an entirely different question. But, the fact remains, you know.

Reading Review

In two or three sentences, write down the point of today's reading.

How does today's reading pertain to you? Give at least two examples.

Can you bring into your life something from today's reading? Write down how you can do that.

Evening Reflection (When in bed)

Review the day in your thoughts. Focus upon what was good today. Think about all that went right. Feel gratitude that things went as well as they did today.

Next, think about those aspects of the day that were less than you wanted them to be. How can you learn from what went wrong today or how can you improve the things you did today? Think about the courage you demonstrated—you did not drink today.

Feel gratitude for another day of sober living.

Day Three—*God Grant Me the Serenity*

Morning Meditation (Upon Rising)

Step Two of A.A. reads, "Came to believe that a Power greater than ourselves could restore us to sanity." Spend this morning's meditation thinking about the meaning of this Step.

Read the Second Step again. Concentrate. What do these words mean to you? Think about this Step and its meaning on both an intellectual and an emotional level.

Thinking About Yourself (Breakfast)

Alcoholics Anonymous is the single most effective way to keep sober. We encourage all alcoholics to make a serious commitment to the Twelve Steps and Twelve Traditions of A.A. By this time, you have been to at least two A.A. meetings and have worked through your initial feelings.

Many people shudder when they hear the name A.A. Their immediate reaction is one of apprehension, anxiety, or fear. Don't be afraid. Alcoholics Anonymous is only a group of people who meet on a regular basis to help each other stay sober. You need this help. There are many fine books, pamphlets, and articles about A.A. From them, learn all you can about A.A. If you want to stay sober, the best way to do it is through regular participation in A.A. meetings and practice of the Twelve Steps of A.A.

For two days we have concentrated on Step One of A.A. Step One of A.A. states, "We admitted we were powerless over alcohol—that our lives had become unmanageable." Before we proceed today, let's review.

Are you powerless over alcohol? Write in your notebook.

How are you powerless over alcohol?

Give three specific examples from your personal life which demonstrate that you are powerless over alcohol.

Is your life unmanageable because of alcohol?

How has your life become unmanageable because of alcohol?

Give three specific examples from your personal life which demonstrate that your life has become unmanageable.

Step One of Alcoholics Anonymous is the cornerstone to recovery. You cannot recover from alcoholism unless you are willing to recognize and accept both the problem itself and the impact of drinking on your life.

Having admitted our alcoholism, we go on to Step Two— "Came to believe that a Power greater than ourselves could restore us to sanity." What does this step mean to you? Write in your notebook.

Describe what you mean by a Power greater than yourself.

How does the phrase "could restore us to sanity" apply to you? How do you interpret this phrase?

Reread Step Two of A.A.—"Came to believe that a Power greater than ourselves could restore us to sanity." Let this Second Step sink in. Do you have any intellectual difficulty accepting this step? If so, what is the difficulty?

How can you apply this step to your recovery from alcoholism?

Emotional Growth (Lunch)

Belief in a Higher Power who can restore us to sanity is both comforting and disquieting. When you stop and think about it, your entire belief system is put on the line with this A.A. step. Especially since, in our culture, spiritual beliefs are unpopular and shunned by many knowledgeable and sophisticated people.

Intellectually, this step may give some recovering alcoholics difficulties. If you have no problem accepting belief in a power greater than yourself and one capable of restoring you to sanity, you are fortunate. If, on the contrary, Step Two causes intellectual difficulty for you, you will need to work harder with this step.

Try to solve this difficulty with your feelings. Do not try to think your way through this step. Feel your way through it. You were able to feel powerless over alcohol. Certainly you can emotionally relate to a Power greater than yourself. Surely you do not see yourself as all-powerful. Read Step Two again.

This time let yourself feel a Power greater than yourself capable of restoring you to sanity. Feel that Power.

Describe your feelings about Step Two of A.A. Write your answer.

Describe your belief that a Power greater than yourself can restore you to sanity. Be specific.

During the day practice recalling the feeling that accompanies your belief in a Power greater than yourself, a Power capable of restoring you to sanity.

Sober Life-Style (Coffee Break)

Step One—"We admitted we were powerless over alcohol—that our lives had become unmanageable."

Step Two—"Came to believe that a Power greater than ourselves could restore us to sanity."

What do these two steps have to do with your life-style? Describe the impact of a commitment to the first two steps. Surely the impact will be greater than a mere decision to stop drinking. What will it be? Write your answer.

You have now been working for three days in this workbook. It is assumed that you are doing all that is requested and not cutting any corners. Good. Sober living requires doing *what* we have to do *when* we have to do it *because* we hold ourselves responsible to do it. In other words, sober living requires self-discipline. Corner-cutting is the opposite of self-discipline.

The next exercise asks you to describe aspects of your life which are good and which you want to retain. All too often, recovering alcoholics see only what they want to change about themselves. They forget to look for good qualities in their old life-style. For example, perhaps even while you were drinking, you always performed your job well. Be careful to be blunt and honest with yourself. Find five qualities of your drinking life which you want to retain in your sober life-style. Write your answers.

Action for the Day (Dinner)

I   Sharing a problem is the first step in solving a problem. Call a close friend (a person other than the one with whom you spend the most time) and share your problem of alcoholism with that person. Even though that person may know you are a recovering alcoholic, call that person and admit that you are powerless over alcohol and that your life has become unmanageable. If you can't find a friend, find someone you trust.

II After your telephone call to your friend, admit to yourself that you are an alcoholic, that you are powerless over alcohol, and that your life is unmanageable. Next, admit that you believe in a Power greater than yourself, one that can restore you to sanity.

III Write Step One of A.A.

IV Write Step Two of A.A.

V   Go to an A.A. meeting. At this meeting, (when it is your turn) say with deep feeling, "My name is _____
(First Name)
and I am an alcoholic."

Feelings: Review of the Day (Beverage Break)

Sharing a problem with a friend, especially, a problem as significant as alcoholism, can be an anxiety-provoking experience. For this reason, people feel they can solve their problems by keeping them to themselves. It is irrational to believe that problems are solved in a vacuum, or that happiness can be achieved by inaction.

If you want something, do what is necessary to get it. When you were practicing your alcoholism, many people knew about it. Some may have tried to help; others may have ignored it. Now that you are treating your alcoholism, ease the burden and share the problem with a friend. After you have done that, describe how you feel now that you have shared your alcoholism with a friend. Use your notebook to answer these questions.

How did you feel when talking to your friend about being powerless over alcohol and living a life that is unmanageable because of alcohol? Write your answer.

How do you feel about having admitted to yourself that you are an alcoholic, that you are powerless over alcohol, and that your life has become unmanageable because of alcohol?

How do you feel after taking Step Two of A.A.: "Came to believe that a Power greater than ourselves could restore us to sanity."

Many of us have difficulty knowing what our feelings really are. Emotional growth and development is an important part of sober living. Do you like yourself?

What do you like about yourself?

How does liking yourself make you feel? Be specific. Write a paragraph about how it feels to like yourself.

Practice arousing a feeling. This may be difficult for you, but try it. Close your eyes. Picture yourself sitting alone on a sandy, warm beach. Hear the waves rolling in? Feel a gentle warm breeze blowing in your face? After you picture yourself sitting on the beach, say to yourself, "I feel good." Let a good feeling flow over your body. Let yourself feel clean, wholesome, and good. Let this feeling run from your toes to your head and back down to your toes again. Describe your feelings in writing. If there are problems with this exercise on the first try, do it again. Describe the experience in your notebook.

Daily Reading (While getting ready for bed)

Doing It For Yourself

Why live soberly? Because your mother asked you to? Because your wife pleads that you not drink? Because your boss has threatened to fire you if you continue to drink? Because a judge told you to sober up? All of these reasons and many more like them may be part of your decision to sober up. But reasons like this will not keep you sober. The only way you can stay sober is to do it for yourself.

What does doing it for yourself mean? It does not mean that the concern and care of others is not good support. On the contrary, the more support and concern that is expressed to the individual practicing sober living, the better are the odds for success. Doing it for yourself means that you have come to grips with the facts; that you are sick and tired of waking up sick and tired.

Doing it for yourself implies having faith and confidence in yourself as a worthwhile person. Many alcoholics feel that everything is lost; that there is no future; that life is hopeless. This is an excuse; it is a way to continue drinking. Life is not over until you are dead. So, instead of dredging up poor excuses about how worthless you are be honest enough to say, "I want to keep drinking."

If you choose sober living, then do it for yourself. You are the most important person. The support of others, especially A.A. and your loved ones, is vital. You need the help of A.A.— you cannot do it alone. On the other hand, you cannot stay sober if you are doing it *for* someone else. You can only stay sober *for* yourself—because you are worth it.

Deciding for sober living does not automatically solve your problems or bring about instant happiness. You must be realistic. You chose sober living because *you* are worth it. But in what ways will sobriety benefit you? Did you opt for sober living to make yourself happy? Or did you decide to practice sober living to reduce your problems?

Most recovering alcoholics choose sober living for both reasons—they want to eliminate problems and they also want to be a little happier. In order to be happy you have to decide upon actions and values and people that make you happy. Then you have to implement a plan of action that allows for the greatest amount of contact with those things that make you happy. This is something that you will have to work on every day.

On the other hand, some of the unhappiness in our lives can be removed. How? By not doing things that make us unhappy. This will require some thought. In essence, what is being proposed is that you identify what makes you unhappy and stop doing it. It's that simple. This does not mean that you will remove all unhappiness from your life. It means that you will be happier because you won't be doing things that make you unhappy.

You decided on sober living for yourself. Take it a step further—decide to live life in as happy a fashion as you can.

Reading Review

In two or three sentences, describe the point of today's reading.

How does today's reading pertain to you? Give at least two examples.

How can you use something from today's reading in your own life? Describe how you can apply today's reading to your life.

Evening Reflection (When in bed)

Review the day in your mind. Think of your accomplishments today.

The most important thing to remember is this: you have been sober for another day. Be grateful. Be proud of yourself and happy that you showed the courage to live another day soberly.

While lying in bed, concentrate on your growth and development in sober living. Say to yourself, "I am doing this for myself. I am happy with myself. I like myself."

Day Four—One Day At A Time

Morning Meditation (Upon Rising)

Step Three of Alcoholics Anonymous reads—"Made a decision to turn our will and our lives over to the care of God *as we understood Him.*" Read this step a second time. Think about what it means. Contemplate the strength and simplicity to be found in this step. If the weather is nice, go outside for a few minutes. Look at the world around you. Meditate on the beauty of nature and the gentle care that nourishes the flowers and the birds. At the end of your meditation try to accept Step Three of A.A.—"Made a decision to turn our will and our lives over to the care of God *as we understood Him.*"

Thinking About Yourself (Breakfast)

Patience. Many alcoholics lack patience. Sober living does not come overnight. Sobriety might. Being dry is simple, you stop drinking. Being sober takes practice and patience. Think about this: "I need patience—NOW!" Sober living is the daily practice of thoughts and actions which, when performed, add up to well-adjusted living. It requires patience, the patience to live soberly every day, day in and day out.

People who are impatient with themselves have an irrational idea. That idea is this: "Things should come to me simply and quickly. If things don't come simply and quickly, they are not worth having." Sober living will not come simply and quickly. It will come steadily over time, but your progress will have peaks and valleys. There will be days when sober living will not seem worth it. There will be days when it is very rewarding. Keep in mind that a person like yourself, who is used to altering the way he thinks and feels with alcohol, will be inclined to "help himself along." You will become impatient with yourself. You will think of many reasons why it would be better to have a drink. The most important quality that you must develop is the ability to take one day at a time. You must be able to tolerate the frustration of practicing something day in and day out—especially when your whole history urges you to have a drink whenever you feel frustrated.

Give yourself a break. You are not God; you're not even a saint. It will take time to develop sober living and it will take time to be comfortable in your new life. Patience will help. Patience is the ability to say to yourself, "I am frustrated because I want it now but instead I have to wait."

Why are you still working on sober living? About this time, many alcoholics become impatient and think of quitting the program. Why are you still working on sober living?

List three reasons in your notebook.

At what age did you start drinking?

When did drinking first become a problem? Give details.

Why did you decide to quit drinking and practice sober living?

Now that you are here and thinking of quitting, where are you going to get the patience to stick to your treatment program? Be specific. How will you keep your thoughts from wandering back to the "good old days"? How will you make yourself practice sober living when you don't feel like it? Patience with yourself has never been your strength. How will you do it now? Will you ask for help from others? Will you go to A.A. meetings? Will you take it one day at a time? Will you do what you have to do? Practice self-discipline? Try to answer all these questions in your notebook.

Emotional Growth (Lunch)

When you become impatient you feel physically uneasy. It frequently starts with twitching or slight sweating. Ordinarily you can feel yourself becoming impatient. Once it starts, deal with the impatience openly. First, label it. Say, "I'm getting impatient with _____ ." (Usually it will be with yourself or another person). Next, share it. Don't keep the feeling bottled up inside. Tell someone you trust that you are impatient. Having identified the feeling and shared it with another person, rethink your reasons for seeking sober living in the first place.

Remember, impatience is irrational. It stems from the misguided belief that everything should come simply and easily after you decide to quit drinking. This kind of thinking allows impatience to grow until you impulsively do something you will later regret.

When you feel yourself becoming impatient with the progress of your recovery, what can you do about it? Be specific. Give examples.

Sober Life-Style (Coffee Break)

Patience does not mean laziness or avoidance of what you have to do. Patience is the ability to do now what can be done now, and to do later what can be done later. Being patient does not mean you can ignore all your other problems because you are dealing with your drinking problem. No, patience is the ability to deal with your alcoholism one day at a time and also deal with your other problems.

What kinds of problems have you had due to drinking? Check them.

Marital	_____	Sexual	_____
Financial	_____	Fighting	_____
Employment	_____	Stealing	_____
Spiritual	_____	Lying	_____
Breaking promises	_____	Cheating	_____
Sneaking drinks	_____	Legal	_____
Drunkenness	_____	Sickness	_____
Accidents	_____	Arguments	_____
Resentments	_____	Hatred	_____
Loneliness	_____	Depression	_____

How has alcoholism made a mess of your life? Be specific on how, when, where and why. Use your notebook.

For all alcoholics the number one problem is alcohol. Alcohol has created most of your problems and alcohol makes other problems more difficult to deal with. It is a vicious circle. Don't lose sight of your primary problem, alcoholism, and spend all your energy on other problems. Consider the anecdote about an alcoholic who kept insisting if he could solve his marital and financial problems he would be OK. Well, he got a divorce and inherited some money, but he wound up drinking that money away and marrying a second woman who created more difficulties than the first.

You must first solve your drinking problem, but at the same time you have to work on your other problems. When you have dealt with your alcoholism it will be easier to take care of other difficulties, or at least to see your other problems through clear eyes and a clear head.

List in your notebook the problems you have right now that are associated with alcohol.

Number the problems in order of importance. Put a #1 next to the biggest problem and a #2 next to the second largest and so on. Write in your notebook.

Now, for each problem, make a plan to solve that problem, as shown below.

1) Name the Problem.
Goal: What you want the solution to be.
Steps to solve the problem: Make a step-by-step plan to solve this problem. What is the first step you have to take to solve this problem? What is the second step?

2) Name the problem.
Goal: What you want the solution to be.
Steps to solve the problem.
Continue this process for all the problems you listed.

Action for the Day (Dinner)

I   Attend an A.A. meeting. Talk at the meeting if you feel like it.

II   Do a favor for someone today. Find someone who needs help and help that person. For example, give someone a ride to the A.A. meeting.

III   Read for half an hour from either the *Big Book* or from the *Twelve Steps and Twelve Traditions*.

Feelings: Review of the Day (Beverage Break)

I   Sometimes when you look at your problems you may become depressed. You may want to roll up in a ball and hide. On the other hand, you may experience a sense of relief when you identify your problems. It may feel as if you are getting something off your chest. Now that you have identified some problems in your life and set some goals to solve these problems, how do you feel? Write in your notebook.

II   Write down how you felt after you'd done a favor for someone. What did you do for the person?

III Do you like the feeling of being able to give to another person? Describe this feeling.

IV   How do you feel when you try to be patient? Is this a good feeling?

V   How do you feel about Step Three of A.A.?—"Made a decision to turn our will and our lives over to the care of God *as we understood Him.*"

Daily Reading (While getting ready for bed)

What Are Your Choices?

If a person decides he is an alcoholic, what choices does he have? Essentially there are two: to drink, or not to drink.

If an alcoholic chooses to return to drinking he should first consider the consequences. The alcoholic always has the option of returning to drinking. No one can take that option away. Only the alcoholic can decide to drink or not to drink. You need to weigh the odds. Face it, most alcoholics do not *want* to stop drinking, they *need* to stop drinking.

What you want versus what you need—this is the personal battle for many people. For the recovering alcoholic, it is the heart of the problem. Alcoholism is a form of self-indulgence. Think of it this way. You *need* to work to support yourself. You *want* to stay out and drink all night. If you do you won't be able to go to work the next morning. What you want versus what you need. You want to spend money on something new, but you need to pay your bills. The whole battle of mature adult living is the battle of doing what you need to do versus what you want to do.

Do you *want* to stay sober? Probably not. Do you *need* to stay sober for your job, your health, your marriage, or yourself? Probably so. What are your choices now that you're sober? They remain the same; to drink or not to drink. Even if you choose to drink, you still have to ask yourself if you can accept the consequences of a return to drinking. Is a return to drinking what you *want*? If you choose to return to drinking, do so only when you know what you are doing and what the probable consequences will be for you. If you choose drinking, do not lie to yourself, or pretend that you can avoid the consequences.

What if you choose not to drink? If you choose to stay sober, you must have reasons for your sobriety. What are your reasons for choosing sober living? All too often the decision to stay sober is made on the basis of temporary conditions (sickness or trouble). If you choose to quit drinking and to begin sober living, it will work only if your decision is based on reasons that will carry you through. A common reason to choose sober living is this: "I want more out of life." The individual with this basis for sobriety can sober up and set out to achieve what he or she wants from life.

Reading Review

In two or three sentences, describe the point of today's reading.

How does today's reading pertain to you? Give at least two examples.

Can you put to work in your life something you learned today? Write down how you can apply today's reading to your life.

Evening Reflection (When in bed)

This morning in meditation, you thought about Step Three of A.A. Tonight concentrate again on this Third Step. Think about how you can apply this step. Step Three—"Made a decision to turn our will and our lives over to the care of God *as we understood Him.*"

Think about this step. How can you turn your will and your life over to the care of God? Also think about the phrase, "God *as we understood Him.*" What does that mean to you?

Day Five—Self-Honesty . . .

Morning Meditation (Upon Rising)

Alone. You may think you are alone in this world. You came into existence alone and will leave this world alone. However, life does not need to be lonely. God is here. Even in our most isolated moments, God is here. You don't need to be alone.

During this morning's meditation, if the weather is agreeable, go outside for a short walk. Contemplate the presence of God in your life. Review in your mind Steps Two and Three of A.A. Step Two—"Came to believe that a Power greater than ourselves could restore us to sanity." Step Three—"Made a decision to turn our will and our lives over to the care of God *as we understood Him.*"

Reaffirm your belief and commitment to these two steps of A.A. Finally, during your morning meditation, feel the presence of God in your life. You are not alone.

Thinking About Yourself (Breakfast)

Honesty is hard enough. Self-honesty can be painful. We all go through life with blinders on. We look at the world selectively so that we can minimize our problems and weak points and maximize our successes and good points.

Alcoholics are especially good at lying to themselves. Many people feel that self-deceit is the core of alcoholism; that you cannot be a practicing alcoholic without telling yourself many lies. The alcoholic's self-lies are usually designed to allow the alcoholic to continue drinking.

This week you admitted to yourself and to others that you are an alcoholic, that you are powerless over alcohol, and that your life was unmanageable due to alcohol. This was probably difficult for you. It required soul-searching, painful honesty, and straightforwardness.

In the past you used a lot of techniques to avoid confronting yourself or to avoid letting others confront you about your alcoholism. These techniques are called denial. By denying his alcoholism, the alcoholic allows himself to continue drinking.

Some common denial techniques are listed below. After each one, write down a specific example of how you used this technique on yourself or on others. Be specific: identify how you denied, lied, conned or manipulated. Use your notebook for this exercise.

1) Outright denial—"I have no problem." Write down an example from your personal life on how you used this defense.

2) Minimizing—Admitting a problem, but discounting its seriousness.

3) Hostility—Defending yourself against those who label you an alcoholic by becoming angry or making threats.

4) Diversion—Changing the subject or dodging issues.

5) Blaming—Pointing a finger or accusing other people, things, or situations for your drinking.

6) Rationalizing—Using excuses or justification for your drinking.

7) Intellectualizing—"Analyzing" the problem, looking for causes, or avoiding personal responsibility for the problem.

Make a list of your three or four most common techniques for denying your drinking problem.

Do you use these denial techniques for other life problems? If so, give an example of each one.

Emotional Growth (Lunch)

Lying is a form of emotional laziness, avoidance, or immaturity. Lying is an attempt to take the easy way out. If you study lying, you will recognize that lies are told when the truth will inconvenience the individual telling the lie. We lie for comfort. We lie when the truth will cause embarrassment, emotional discomfort or a consequence we wish to avoid.

Many people believe that alcoholism is maintained by lies—both self-lies and lies to other people. Early on in the alcoholic process, the individual becoming alcoholic avoids the consequences of his drinking by lying.

In recovering from alcoholism, one of the initial steps requires telling the truth: "I am an alcoholic, I am powerless over alcohol, my life is unmanageable due to alcohol." However, this is just the beginning. Recovery requires more than identification of the truth—it requires eliminating all the ways that we learned to avoid the truth: lies, minimizing, hostility, diversion, blaming, rationalizing, intellectualizing, changing the topic.

When you told lies in the past to cover up some action or lack of action, how did you feel afterwards? Describe your emotional reaction to the lies you told. Write in your notebook.

How will you feel in the future when you do away with all the lying? In other words, if you had to use the truth at all times in the future, how would you feel? How would it affect your life? Would you feel hemmed in?

Sober Life-Style (Coffee Break)

To develop a sober life-style, you need to develop the habit of telling the truth. Telling the truth will be easier the more you understand your lying.

To whom do you lie? Make a list of people to whom you have lied most frequently. Think about your spouse, children, parents, friends, and employer. Make a list of at least six people. Write in your notebook.

What kind of lies do you tell? Be specific. How do you profit by lying? What happens when you lie to yourself or to others? Write it down.

When are you most likely to lie? Think of the times you've lied. Do they usually occur when you've been drinking? When you're tired? When you feel lazy? Be specific and think about the times when you lie.

Where do you lie? Anywhere? At work? At home?

Why do you lie? Do you lie to avoid the issue or to acquire something? Mention at least three different kinds of lies you tell.

Now that you have looked at the who, what, when, where and why of the lies you told, what general conclusion can you make about your lies?

What do you think you need to do, think or say in order to break this pattern? Write your answers.

How can you develop a pattern of telling the truth? How will you remind yourself? How will you catch yourself when you're not telling the truth?

Action for the Day (Dinner)

I   Practice telling the blunt and straightforward truth. The truth will set you free.

II   Go to an A.A. meeting. If the opportunity arises, talk about how you used denial to continue drinking.

III   Share with someone you don't know too well—perhaps someone after the A.A. meeting—your three or four most common forms of denial and what you plan to do to eliminate them.

Feelings: Review of the Day (Beverage Break)

I   A person prepares himself to return to drinking by manipulating the truth. Some common methods are:

   a) Lying, with outright denial of what is known to be true.

   b) Blaming others for one's own shortcomings or mistakes.

   c) Minimizing or maximizing problems.

   d) Assuming people are against you or out to get you.

   e) Nursing guilt feelings or depression over past wrongdoings.

   f) Feeling helpless or overwhelmed, with no way to solve your problem.

How does looking at your denial techniques make you feel? Write in your notebook. How did you feel telling another person about your use of denial to allow yourself to continue drinking?

II   Sometimes telling other people the truth, especially people close to us, makes us feel trapped or hemmed in. This feeling is natural because when we tell others how we manipulated the truth in the past we reduce the possibility of doing the same in the future. If we are totally blunt and honest about how we distorted the truth to suit ourselves, we lessen the chance of deceiving the same person again.

The purpose of this exercise is to burn bridges. If we eliminate or reduce the number of people we can manipulate then we reduce the possibility of a return to drinking. If you feel trapped, so be it; this is part of the price you pay for sober living. Eventually the good feeling of sober living will take away this feeling of being trapped.

If you want to set yourself free of denial, pick out the two people you lied to most. Probably a spouse, a friend or an employer. If you want to feel honesty, call that person or, if you can, see them face to face and explain how you lied to them to cover up your alcoholism. Practice honesty, talk to these two people *now*—then come back to the workbook.

How does honesty feel? Write in your notebook.

What were your emotional reactions when you told these people about lying? Were you nervous, angry, depressed? Write out your answers.

III Having worked on honesty for most of the day, now practice feeling good. Sit in a quiet place. Close your eyes. Take a few deep breaths and exhale slowly. As you sit alone, picture yourself on a quiet sandy beach. Listen to the waves breaking softly in the background. Think about being clean. Feel wholesome. Allow your spirits to rise. See yourself actually soar away. Feeling good? Happy with yourself? Say to yourself, "I am a good person. I am sober."

Daily Reading (While getting ready for bed)

Sober Living

Sober living is more than sobriety. This is not just hair-splitting. There is a very important distinction to make here; a distinction that you will need to understand if treatment is to be successful.

Sobriety is life without drinking. Sobriety is the foundation of sober living. Sobriety is day in and day out avoidance of alcoholic beverages. This in itself is a difficult chore and will require a lot of work and attention.

Sober living, on the other hand, is a happy, productive life without alcohol. You can see that sober living rests on a foundation of sobriety. Sober living takes sobriety beyond abstinence to personal growth and happiness. Sober living comes from A.A. attendance and practice of the Twelve Steps.

Sober living first starts with a well-balanced life. We are biological creatures first, and we need to take care of our bodies if we are to achieve sober living. Sober living requires sufficient rest, exercise, and nutritious food. When you finish this workbook you should see your physician for a checkup. Discuss with your doctor your plan to improve your health. Ask him about diet and exercise. Be specific. Call for an appointment and tell the receptionist you would like a physical and that you would like to schedule time (about fifteen minutes) to talk to the physician about your health plans. Be prepared for this discussion. Bring notes. Jot down your questions ahead of time so you won't forget. Also have a plan for developing your physical condition. Show it to your physician. Then implement your plan for physical conditioning.

The next step after physical health is mental health. Just as drinking ordinarily deteriorates your physical health alcoholism also undermines your mental health. After you have been sober for some time, take an inventory of your mental health. Do you have problems with emotions? Are you depressed, irritable or tense? Do you harbor grudges and resentments? Is your thinking as clear and objective as you would like? We will spend many pages in this workbook helping you to assess your mental health and teaching you to deal with these problems. If you find that your mental health is not sufficiently improved by this workbook, perhaps you should seek professional help. Be sure to inform the professional that you are a recovering alcoholic. Do not rely on tranquilizers to solve your problems. You must learn new ways of living and problem-solving.

Next, sober living requires secure financial planning. You can't survive long in this world without the ability to pay your way. Sound fiscal planning requires an income. Unless you are planning to get another job, sober living requires that you secure the job you now have. That means doing the work well. It means relating well to the supervisors and fellow-workers.

It means developing the job into a good, secure place to work.

If the job is secure and you are satisfied with the work, review your spending. Do you live within your means? Are you saving anything for a rainy day? We will review all of this later in the workbook and develop plans to solve any problems.

The final concerns of sober living include responsibilities, social activities, spiritual life, and recreation. An individual practicing sober living does what is necessary to live success- fully. In future sections we will review all the ingredients of sober living and help you to develop plans of action for each area of your life that is not well-balanced.

Sobriety is the absence of alcohol. If you don't drink then you are sober. Sober living on the other hand, is a healthy approach to life. It is more than avoiding alcohol. It is doing in a systematic way those things that are necessary for a happy and productive life. The practice of sober living is a uniquely personal program. No two people live the same way; therefore, no two people will practice sober living in the same way. Each person must individually decide what sober living means. The question is, "What do you need to do to make your life better?"

Sober living is a daily commitment to a life without alcohol and to those things that improve our lives. This may sound like a pie-in-the-sky cliche. It isn't. Sober living is nothing more than taking charge of your life in such a way that the quality of your life is improved.

Sober living is doing what you have to do to be happy. It is not merely doing what you want to do. Sometimes what you want to do conflicts with what you need to do. We will spend time helping you develop a sober living plan; a plan of life that will allow you to accomplish your goals. A sober living plan does not enslave you but rather frees you to do all you must do and still have free time. Remember the proverb, "All work and no play makes Johnny a dull boy." Similarly, sober living is a healthy combination of what we *need* to do with what we *want* to do. Many people who practice sober living reward themselves with special privileges for accomplishing what needs to be done, especially if it is an exceptionally difficult chore.

Sober living does not make life easy. On the contrary, sober living requires that you do the things you have to do but don't like to do. Sober living requires that you meet your responsibilities first then do the things you enjoy. You reward yourself for successful accomplishment.

Sobriety is the first step for the alcoholic. Sobriety is abstinence from alcohol. Sober living goes beyond sobriety. Sober living is best achieved by A.A. involvement and by organizing all the components of your life in an orderly way. It is doing what you *need* to do first; then doing what you *want* to do. Finally, sober living is the practice of life in a mature, responsible, productive manner that leads to a lifetime of happiness.

Reading Review

In two or three sentences, describe the point of today's reading.

How is today's reading relevant to your life? Give at least two examples.

Can you apply something from today's reading to your own life? How?

Evening Reflection (When in bed)

Review your progress so far. Think about the good you have accomplished. Realize that what you have done so far has been by your own choice. You have come this far in sober living. Compliment yourself. Praise yourself for what you have done. Also, renew your commitment to sober living.

Spend a few minutes reflecting upon the assistance you have received. Be grateful to your Higher Power for the help you have received. Feel grateful to the people who have helped you. Think of ways you can demonstrate your gratitude.

Day Six—*The Truth Will Set You Free . . .*

Morning Meditation (Upon Rising)

For a few moments allow all the stress and strain of yesterday as well as all the anticipation about today to be placed aside. Push extraneous thoughts from your mind. Strive for inner peace.

Feel content with yourself. Allow your spirit to soar. Let the peace of God flow into your heart. Let this feeling take over your entire being. Feel inner peace. Let God's peace set you free; free to be happy; free to love and share with others; free to be well and whole today.

Thinking About Yourself (Breakfast)

Sober living requires constant attention to the truth. Truth is illusive. Sometimes we don't know how we feel; how we think; why we do what we do or say what we say. Usually, things in life happen so fast that we don't have time to uncover the truth.

Know yourself. Know your strengths and weaknesses. If you know yourself you know the truth. If you live a life consistent with the truth you will not drink.

Alcoholism is a form of lying. The alcoholic develops a way of life to hide the truth, and hiding the truth is lying.

Common lies of the alcoholic are listed below. Give a personal example for each type of lie. Be brutally honest with yourself. Write your answers.

Breaking promises.

Pretending to be sober when you're drunk.

Blackouts; pretending to remember events when you don't.

Minimizing drinking, telling another person or telling yourself you drink no more than other people do.

Lying to self; truly believing that your drinking was not out of control when it really was.

Tremors; hiding your hands from another person because they trembled, or hiding other harmful effects of your drinking from other people.

Frequent intoxication; telling someone you rarely get drunk when the truth was different.

Morning drinking; drinking at unusual times and hiding the fact from another person.

Substituting alcohol for food by telling someone you weren't really hungry after all.

Sickness; saying you had the flu, or some other acceptable illness, when the fact was you were hungover or sick from drinking.

Avoidance; having someone else call your boss to say you were too sick to come to the phone, when the fact was you were too afraid or embarrassed.

Picking a fight with your wife or someone else as an excuse to drink.

Nervousness; saying you were nervous when the fact was you were either hungover or craving a drink.

Gift giving; being extravagant with gifts or affection when the fact was you were feeling guilty about drinking.

Hiding bottles; pretending to go to another room or some other place for a "good" reason when the fact is you were nipping on a bottle there.

Make a list of ten lies you told to cover or defend your drinking. Do not use any of the specific examples you've already used. Force yourself to find the lies. Write them down.

Emotional Growth (Lunch)

For the past two days we have concentrated on how your lies, both to yourself and to others, have maintained your alcoholism. Many recovering alcoholics feel guilty, depressed, or anxious when they look at how they have deceived themselves and others. Sometimes feelings of shame, embarrassment or social awkwardness emerge after studying our lies and how they affect others.

Ordinarily, there is an emotional reaction to the honest study of one's deceptions. What is your emotional reaction to reviewing the role of lies in your life? Write a specific answer.

Like most emotions, your emotional reaction to reviewing

your lying is neither good nor bad. How you deal with these emotions, what you do with them or how they affect your future life is what is important. How will your emotional reaction to recognizing your lies affect your telling of lies in the future? Will there be an effect? Will it cause you to avoid telling lies in the future? Write a specific answer.

Telling the truth is essential to recovering from alcoholism. It is also essential to developing a well-balanced emotional life. Extreme feelings of guilt and shame will be avoided the more we tell the truth. Sober living is the practice of what we have to do when we have to do it. Sober living is the practice of truth. The more we practice truth the more we will grow, not only in our recovery from alcoholism, but in our emotional lives as well.

Sober Life-Style (Coffee Break)

Learning to tell the truth is not accidental or haphazard. To achieve the habit of telling the truth you need a plan of action. Now that you are sober many of the reasons for your lies will be gone. However, there will still be a need to remind yourself daily, especially in the little things. Remember, you didn't start out as a full-blown alcoholic; it took time and practice. It was the avoidance of truth, responsibility and commitment that prepared you to lie and to keep drinking. You got into the habit of taking the easy way out. Now you have to develop the habit of truth; which is the harder way. How will you remind yourself to do this?

Develop an honesty plan. First decide that the practice of telling the truth daily will strengthen your sober living. Next print the word TRUTH on a 3x5 card and tape it to your bathroom mirror. Each morning while grooming remind yourself of the value of practicing the truth. Each evening, review your success at the truth habit. On days when you do not do well, reprimand yourself and resolve to renew the truth habit.

Like any habit, the truth habit takes time to develop. If you make a concentrated effort to practice the truth each day you will achieve a healthy habit of telling the truth.

One last word about the truth habit. There are two reasons for telling the truth: a) to eliminate the lies to yourself and lies to others that allowed you to drink, and b) to eliminate the emotional distress that lying brought and to establish the emotional equilibrium that truth brings. The truth habit is for self-development; it will make you more secure; you will feel better about yourself.

Write down your plan to develop the truth habit. Be specific. How will you check on yourself? How will you monitor progress?

Action for the Day (Dinner)

I   Go to an A.A. meeting. If possible, describe the way you used lies to maintain your drinking.

II   Lying becomes second nature to the alcoholic. In the recovery process, each alcoholic needs a plan to tell the truth. It is easier to learn to tell the truth to others than it is to tell the truth to ourselves. Sometimes we lie to ourselves without knowing that we are lying.

These are usually little lies. Here are a few examples. "I'll stop at my favorite bar to buy a pack of cigarettes." "I'll stop at the bar to have a coke." "I'll have just one beer." "One beer can't hurt." Review your plan for developing the truth habit. Make sure your plan makes clear how you will practice honesty with yourself as well as with others.

III   Call your spouse (or a parent, brother or sister, or close friend). During the conversation be totally honest, be blunt, and tell this person about your need to have an honesty plan. Tell this person all about your honesty plan.

Feelings: Review of the Day (Beverage Break)

I   How do you feel when you think about the lies you've told? Write your answers in your notebook. How did you feel talking to your spouse about your honesty plan? How do you feel about an honesty plan?

II   Practice feeling good. Find a quiet place for yourself. Close your eyes and remove all distractions from your mind.

Say to yourself, "My life is improving; I'm sober; I'm telling the truth and I'm working on my problems." Feel good. Feel some self-pride. Think worthwhile thoughts about yourself.

When you feel good, where do you feel it? Describe the sensation of feeling good.

Daily Reading (While getting ready for bed)

What Is Alcoholism?

Alcoholism is a disease. This disease is progressive and chronic. It manifests itself in disturbances of the mind and body, and is characterized by behavior disorders. Once the alcoholic starts drinking, he may be no more able to control his compulsion to continue drinking than an individual with tuberculosis is able to voluntarily control the coughing reflex.

Alcoholism is a disease. Alcoholism erodes and destroys health, job, family, friendship, and soul. This disease creates most of the problems the alcoholic experiences. Alcoholism is the misuse of alcoholic beverages. Alcoholism is the drinking of alcoholic beverages irresponsibly.

Alcoholism is a social problem because it destroys the alcoholic's relationship with others. Alcohol is a demanding social partner. The more time you spend with alcohol, the more of your time alcohol consumes. It dissolves the alcoholic's social life into a lonely pair—the drunk and the bottle.

Alcoholism is moral and spiritual bankruptcy. Because of the deceit, manipulation and distortion of reality by the alcoholic, his moral and spiritual values gradually erode. The alcoholic finds himself in "the dark night of the soul." His values have slipped away. What is left is a belief in alcohol as the solution to all problems. Alcohol is an ugly and demanding god. The more homage the alcoholic pays to this false god, the more morally and spiritually bankrupt, alone, and meaningless he becomes.

No one becomes an alcoholic overnight. This illness takes time. It also takes practice to become an alcoholic. One slowly develops the pattern of misusing alcohol. As this disease gets worse it interferes with sleep and eating. The misuse of alcohol, along with the interruption of sleeping and eating patterns, causes all kinds of physical stress and illness. It is at this point that the habit of alcohol misuse, the constant state of physical fatigue and emotional stress, causes us to lie to ourselves and hide from the fact that our drinking is harming us. Lying is the beginning of moral erosion. Lying, either to self or others, enables the alcoholic to maintain his drinking and to ignore the cause of his physical discomfort. All of these things taken together demand more and more of his time and take him away from his employment and social and family commitments.

Reading Review

This section is designed to develop your ability to apply what you read.

In two or three sentences, describe the point of today's reading.

How does today's reading pertain to you? Give at least two examples.

Can you apply something from today's reading to your life? How?

Evening Reflection (When in bed)

Tonight contemplate Step One of A.A.—"We admitted we were powerless over alcohol—that our lives had become unmanageable." Feel the full impact of this statement. Spend the next few moments realizing and reviewing how far you have come in your recovery from alcoholism. Finally, feel grateful to God and all the individuals in your life who helped you come this far.

Day Seven—*Make Yourself Happy* . . .

Morning Meditation (Upon Rising)

Look at the world around you. If the weather permits, go for a walk this morning. If not, look out the window. Get in touch with nature; look at the natural beauty around you. Feel good about yourself and about your world. Feel the spirit and strength of God flowing through all that natural beauty. Perform an act of gratitude for having this moment alone, for being alive and being able to share in the beauty that exists in the universe.

You are sober.

Thinking About Yourself (Breakfast)

Happiness does not happen accidentally. You have to work at being happy. Think about what you have accomplished this week. You have stayed sober. Even though this is probably not the first time you've tried to stay sober, this time you have done so by practicing sober living. Second, you have begun to look at your life honestly. The truth, whether painful or beautiful, will be the foundation of your new life.

You have worked hard this week. You have begun to develop the groundwork for a successful, sober, happy life. Maybe you feel happy, maybe you don't.

What did you do yesterday to make yourself happy? If you did nothing, explain why. Write your answers in your notebook.

Happiness sometimes depends upon how you think about certain things. What do you think about:

1) Finishing one week of sober living?
2) Telling the truth?
3) Giving up drinking?
4) Improving your life?
5) Problems in your life?
6) Happiness?

In the observations you made above, you could have looked at things that make you happy or you could have ignored those things and seen only things that make you unhappy. The choice is yours.

Emotional Growth (Lunch)

What is happiness? Is it getting everything you want when you want it? Is it freedom from pain and discomfort? Is it utopia or heaven on earth?

What is happiness for you? Write in your notebook.

Review your answer to the question above. If your answer focuses upon fleeting emotional states, then remember the little girl who said she loved steak and that having steak made her very happy—until she had it every day for a month. At the end of the month, steak didn't make her so happy.

Happiness is difficult to define. It is best to define happiness in terms of actions rather than feelings. For example, "Happiness is a job which keeps me busy, in which I'm interested, and from which I achieve a sense of accomplishment," rather than, "Happiness is feeling good all over." There are two reasons for taking a functional, action-oriented approach. First, you can define an action, and second, you can do it. That's right, you can do the things that make you happy.

Write another answer to the question, "What is happiness for you?" This time define happiness in terms of things you can do to make yourself happy.

What actions make you happy? Write them down.

Do you routinely do the things that make you happy? If so, does it work? Are you happy?

Being sober does not mean automatic happiness. When the alcoholic sobers up he often has to deal with problems which drinking allowed him to ignore. This may cause distress and unhappiness. So be it. That is part of the price you pay for sober living.

Happiness is another matter. It has to be worked on as much as sober living. It helps your sober living if the things that make you happy and the things that keep you sober are the same. If not, do what keeps you sober then add activities that make you happy.

Sober Life-Style (Coffee Break)

Review what you've learned this week about yourself, your drinking and your life. List at least ten items in your notebook.

How do these observations affect your living? In other words, what changes have you made in your life because of what you've learned this week? Make a list of these changes.

You have completed almost one week of sober living. Write a paragraph or two entitled: *How I Intend To Live What I've Learned This Week.*

Action for the Day (Dinner)

I Go to an A.A. meeting. If you have the opportunity to speak, tell the group what you have accomplished this week.

II *Do* something today to make yourself happy. Complete the *action* that you enjoy doing.

III *Do* something to make someone else happy. Complete an *action* of a giving nature which makes another person happy.

Feelings: Review of the Day (Beverage Break)

I How does happiness feel? Describe it. Write down your answer. What did you *do* to make yourself happy today? What *action* did you perform? Was it successful? Why?

What did you *do* to make someone else happy today? Was it successful?

Make a list of ten actions that make you happy.

II If sober living isn't better than drunk living then why live soberly? Sometimes individuals sober up and expect instant happiness. That won't happen, and that attitude won't lead to sober living.

If you want your sober life to be happy, you will have to work at it. You have developed a list of ten actions that make you happy. There is no magic to it. If you want to be happy *do* those things which make you happy.

III Practice feeling good. Conjure up the thoughts or images
you need to bring on a feeling of being good, wholesome
and healthy.

Were you successful at feeling good about yourself? How
can you improve your ability to bring on this feeling?

Daily Reading (While getting ready for bed)

Thinking of Drinking

This happens to every recovering alcoholic. There comes
the day, the time, when all you think about is drinking. These
days prove the truth of Step One, "powerlessness." All your
reasons to be sober will seem insufficient to keep thoughts of
drinking out of your head. You will be doing something and
suddenly realize you are thinking of drinking.

What is thinking of drinking? Usually it is not a deliberate
act. Ordinarily, it sneaks up on you. You'll be busy doing
something and all of a sudden find yourself remembering a
good time you had at a particular bar or during a particular
drinking episode. Sometimes thinking of drinking and an
impulse to drink come together but they are different phe-
nomena. An impulse to drink is a call to action. Thinking of
drinking usually is limited to thinking about past drinking
events or how you can get away with future drinking.

Thinking of drinking is similar to a haunting melody or tune
which goes through your head over and over again. We've all
had the experience of hearing a catchy tune, enjoying it, and
then sometime later, this tune pops up in our memory like a
record going round and round. At those times we found that
the more we concentrated on getting rid of the repeated
melody, the more aware of it we were and the more pronounced
it seemed.

Thinking of drinking is like a tune stuck in your head.
Many alcoholics say it can almost drive them to drink. The first
thing you must do is to distinguish between thinking about
future drinking and thinking about past drinking.

Thinking about future drinking is planning to drink, because when we think about future drinking we see all the reasons why we can have a few drinks and minimize all the reasons why we cannot drink. It's amazing how the mind can prepare us to drink. We actually fool ourselves into believing that we can handle booze; that we can limit our drinking. This phenomenon is not uncommon. When we remember the past, we tend to glorify the good and minimize the bad.

It is thinking of past drinking and remembering the relief, the pleasure or the fun that sets us up to think that we can drink again. It would be a lie to say that we never had fun while drinking. The fact is that drinking has a lot of pleasurable events associated with it. It is these events that we remember, and we forget the tragic consequences.

When you find yourself thinking of drinking, when there is a haunting, nagging thought about drinking, this is the time to go to an A.A. meeting. The A.A. meeting won't necessarily remove the thought of drinking, but it will help you focus on why you chose to be sober.

Another way to deal with thoughts of drinking is to have a daily thinking plan. If you spend fifteen minutes in the morning in meditation and fifteen minutes in the evening in meditative reflection, thoughts of drinking will be minimized.

How do you meditate? Essentially, one meditates by sitting in a quiet room and thinking. What do you think about? Yourself, your life, the day ahead. There are many books on meditation. Two of the best, written by recovering alcoholics are called, *Day By Day* and *Twenty-Four Hours a Day*. They can be of great assistance in your meditations. Get copies and use them.

Reflection is a quiet unwinding. It is thinking about the day; reviewing your progress and actions. Reflection includes a review of today's activities and some preview of tomorrow's.

Thoughts of drinking will occur to all recovering alcoholics. They are best handled by realizing that this kind of thinking is a preparation to drink, and an A.A. meeting is in order. Secondly, if you practice meditation and reflection regularly, you will minimize the effect of thoughts of drinking.

Reading Review

In two or three sentences, describe the point of today's reading.

How does today's reading pertain to you? Give at least two examples.

Can you apply something from today's reading to your life? How?

Evening Reflection (When in bed)

You have completed one week of your sober living program. You have worked hard and you have learned a lot about yourself. Let that thought sink in: you *are* learning sober living. Review what you have accomplished and give yourself credit for it. Also remember that you did not do it alone. Be grateful to your Higher Power and all those people who helped you achieve this initial week of sober living.

During your prayer and reflection, ask for the help, guidance and courage to continue to do all that keeps you sober.

Prologue to Week Two

Sober living is many things to many people, but there is one thing it is not, it is not easy.

Sober living requires constant vigilance and reformation of goals. Having completed one week of this program, you have some idea of what sober living will entail for you.

What is the price of sober living? At treatment programs a client will often be asked, "What are you willing to pay for your sober living?" What they are talking about is the cost in work, time, action, feeling, thinking, and friendship. This is the true cost of sober living.

Sober living is not a simple case of putting the plug in the jug, swearing off booze, and living happily ever after. No. There is a price that must be paid for sober living; the price is change.

Sober living, like getting an "A" in a course, will involve hard work. It will take planning, practice, and more practice. You will not be able to cut corners, take the easy way out, or avoid the truth.

This week we will focus on learning to live soberly. What are you willing to do to get a good grade in sober living?

Let's review what you have accomplished to date:

1) You admitted that you are an alcoholic.
2) You realized that drinking is the source of your problem and that the solution is to stop drinking and start sober living.
3) You have accepted both of the above statements by taking Step One of A.A.: "We admitted we were powerless over alcohol—that our lives had become unmanageable."
4) You learned that your alcoholism was fostered by lies to yourself and that honesty and integrity are essential to recovery from your alcoholism.
5) You learned of the fellowship of A.A.

6) You recognized your spiritual needs by accepting Steps Two and Three of A.A.:

Step Two—"Came to believe that a Power greater than ourselves could restore us to sanity."

Step Three—"Made a decision to turn our will and our lives over to the care of God, *as we understood Him.*"

7) You have established the pattern of always telling the truth to yourself and to others.

During Week II, follow the workbook as systematically as possible. You may have to adjust the times of certain exercises, but make an effort to do each one according to your personal schedule. Once you have decided upon your schedule, stick to it. The schedule below is only an example.

Workbook Exercises	Optional Schedule	Daily Routine
Morning Meditation	6:30 a.m.	Upon Rising
Thinking About Yourself	8:00 a.m.	Breakfast
Emotional Growth	12:00 p.m.	Lunch
Sober Life-Style	3:00 p.m.	Coffee Break
Action for the Day	6:00 p.m.	Dinner
Feelings: Review of the Day	9:00 p.m.	Beverage Break
Daily Reading	11:00 p.m.	While getting ready for bed
Evening Reflection	11:30 p.m.	When in bed

The importance of doing each exercise on a schedule is to establish a rhythm to your sober living. Things will come up that will seem to make it impossible to stick to your schedule. Challenge yourself; it can be done. It is important to gain the ability to get things done when they have to be done.

Your A.A. program so far:

1) "We admitted we were powerless over alcohol—that our lives had become unmanageable."

2) "Came to believe that a Power greater than ourselves could restore us to sanity."

3) "Made a decision to turn our will and our lives over to the care of God *as we understood Him.*"

Day Eight—*Easy Does It . . .*

Morning Meditation (Upon Rising)

Congratulations, you are starting your second week of sober living. There is a distinction between sobriety and sober living. Sobriety is the absence of alcohol. Sober living is not only the absence of alcohol, but the habit of thinking, feeling and acting in a healthy, productive, problem-solving fashion.

Sobriety alone will work for a while. Sober living is a life-style that will carry you for the rest of your life, if you practice it daily.

Meditate this morning on your sober living; focus on the quality of your life. Give thanks to your Higher Power for all that is good in you and in your life. As you spend time thinking about the good aspects of your sober life, review some of them and think about how you can improve the quality of your sober living.

Thinking About Yourself (Breakfast)

What does sober living mean to you? Write in your notebook.

Sober living is essentially well-balanced living. Well-balanced living starts with sufficient rest, nutrition, and work. These three activities consume two-thirds of our working day. During the remaining eight hours of each work day and the approximately sixteen hours on Saturday and Sunday, we have to develop sufficient participation in other essential areas of our lives. These include: A.A., recreation, and church (personal spiritual development for those who do not attend church). We need to include our family and friends in our recreation. We need time to do chores such as shopping, cooking, and cleaning. Sober living is well-balanced living; it is the right amount of each essential activity.

Essential Life Activities
1) Work
2) Sleep
3) Food

   4) Exercise
   5) A.A. meetings
   6) Recreation
   7) Spiritual development
   8) Family activities
   9) Friends
   10) Chores

The right proportion of each of these activities adds up to a well-balanced sober life.

Some areas of your life are unbalanced. Others are already well-balanced. The fact that you are an alcoholic does not necessarily mean that your entire life is in shambles. As you put your life back in order, it is always good to know what your assets are.

In this next section of the workbook, go through each of the ten essential areas of life and write down how you already accomplish these activities. While doing this section, keep in mind that you are accentuating the positive, well-balanced actions in your life.

1) **Work**

Most people spend the greatest part of their waking hours engaged in some kind of work. People who enjoy their work tend to lead happy lives. However, many people feel trapped by their jobs. They feel they cannot get a job that pays well and can do nothing to improve their job situation. People with alcohol problems need to take a serious look at their jobs. There are many job problems caused by alcoholism, but other problems may be due to other factors. Both kinds of problems need to be examined.

If you want to be happy, you must work at a job which you enjoy and one which pays well enough to meet your needs.

What is good about your job? Write your answer.

Do you work six to ten hours daily, five days per week? Do you have sufficient income to support your life-style? Are you happy at your job?

Does your job have health insurance and a retirement plan?

Do you get along with co-workers?

Do you get along with job supervisors?

What is bad about your job?

How can you improve your job?

Make a plan to improve your job situation. Make sure the plan is well-balanced; that it includes six to ten working hours per day, mental and physical stimulation, good work relationships, sufficient pay and fringe benefits. In your plan, identify the aspects of your work life which you are going to improve and set out the steps you can take to improve them.

2) Sleep

People vary in how much sleep they need. Most adults need between six and eight hours per day. Many recovering alcoholics suffer from a sleep disturbance pattern. They have problems getting to sleep, or problems with fitful, disturbed sleep, or problems with waking up exhausted.

Healthy well-balanced living rests on well-balanced sleep patterns. People with sleep disturbance patterns should practice going to bed at the same time seven nights a week. They should practice staying in bed until it is time to get up and always getting up at the same time every day. Read for half an hour before bed time. Drink no coffee or other caffeine beverages after 6:00 p.m. Follow this schedule every day. It will work if you practice it.

Most people who have sleep disturbance problems don't stick to a schedule. They nap during the day, read or watch T.V. when they can't sleep and allow themselves to go to bed or get up when they feel like it.

Do you sleep six to eight hours a day?

Do you get sufficient rest?

Is your sleep fitful and disturbed?

What are the problems with your sleep? Write in your notebook.

Write down a plan of action that will develop well-balanced sleep practices.

3) **Food**

Most practicing alcoholics ignore their eating habits. Alcoholics are often malnourished.

The recovering alcoholic needs to eat three meals per day. Even when you don't feel like it, practice eating three times per day. Don't snack, except perhaps at night when relaxing. Learn about nutrition and eat three well-balanced meals. Practice eating fruits, vegetables, and cereals along with meat and starches. Eat your meals at the same time every day.

Food is what we live on; the body needs nutrition. If you are concerned about your nutrition, consult your family physician. Remember that overeating is as bad as not eating enough.

What is good about your eating habits? Write in your notebook.

Do you eat three meals a day?

Do you snack too much?

Are your meals well-balanced?

Do you eat enough fruits and vegetables?

Do you eat either too much or too little?

Make a plan of action to establish a well-balanced eating plan. Be specific.

4) **Exercise**

Alcoholics are not the only people who don't get enough exercise, but because your physical condition has deteriorated because of your alcoholism it is especially important for you to develop a regular exercise plan. It is wise to consult your family physician when developing a plan for physical exercise. There are many fine books on the market dealing with physical fitness.

The important thing is not how hard you exercise but that you do it regularly. People who play five sets of tennis on weekends would do better to play two sets of tennis on alternating days.

What is good about the level of exercise in your life? Write in your notebook.

Do you do organized daily exercise?

Do you walk instead of ride when you can?

Do you take stairs instead of taking an elevator when it is only a flight or two?

Do you go for walks?

What can you do to improve your exercise life?

Write out a plan for a life with a better exercise program. Make sure this plan is well-balanced. Don't overdo it. Consult your family physician. Practice your exercise schedule daily. Remember, it is better to do a little bit of exercise on a regular daily basis than to do a lot of exercise once in a while.

5) A.A. Meetings

Attendance at A.A. is the single best way to help maintain sobriety. A.A. is good for you as long as you keep it in balance. Some recovering alcoholics get so involved in A.A. they forget other aspects of their lives. Other recovering alcoholics don't get sufficiently involved in A.A. They go to the meetings, but they don't get involved or don't commit themselves to the program.

For A.A. to be effective, you need to be an active listener and an open and honest speaker. Listen to what others have to say and express what you think and feel. Also, find a sponsor, a person who has several years of successful living through A.A. participation. Pick a home group that is both convenient and comfortable. Finally, attend at least two A.A. meetings each week for the first year of your sober life.

What is good about A.A. attendance? Write your answers in your notebook.

Do you listen to and evaluate what others say?

Do you try to apply what others have to say in your life?

Do you speak what you are thinking and feeling at A.A. meetings?

Are you comfortable with the people you've met at A.A.?

Do you perform any volunteer activities at A.A. such as making the coffee?

What is bad about your A.A. experience?

How can you improve your A.A. experience?

Make a plan for a better A.A. experience. Be sure the plan

is well-balanced. That is, attend at least two meetings a week, pick a home group, and find people you enjoy being around. Visit different A.A. groups if necessary. In your A.A. plan, identify the aspect of your A.A. experience you hope to improve. Specify how you are going to improve it. Set out the steps you will take to improve your A.A. life. Write all of this down.

6) **Recreation**

Recreation is one of the most ignored or overlooked areas of daily living. Healthy living requires a certain amount of time spent in recreation. How much time you spend, and in what activities you spend it is up to you. However, most people don't plan their recreation and spend more time doing nothing than they would like.

Make a list of those activities which you enjoy most. The list should include routine recreational activities such as watching T.V., reading the paper and playing with the children. After you've made a list of these activities, decide how much time you would like to spend on each of them. Write your list now.

Next, make a list of those occasional recreational activities that you like, such as going to the movies, going out for dinner or swimming. After you've completed this list, try to decide how frequently you would like to engage in each activity.

You will probably find that you have more things to do than you have time for. You will probably also realize that drinking consumed great amounts of your time.

What is good about your current recreational life? Write out your answers.

Do you recreate two to four hours a day?

Do you have a sufficient variety of recreational activities?

Are you happy with your recreational activities?

What is bad about your recreational life?

How can you improve the quality of your recreational activities?

Make a plan for better recreational satisfaction. Make sure the plan is well-balanced; that it fills two to four hours a day, offers interesting and rewarding activities and has sufficient variety to maintain your interest. In your plan, identify the activities, the people, the places and the times for recreation. Also identify the safeguards you will build into your plan to keep you active and happy.

7) Spiritual Development

Spiritual development is ignored by many recovering alcoholics. In order to be happy, everyone needs a sense of values, purpose and integrity. This does not necessarily mean participation in an organized religion. Some recovering alcoholics who do participate in religious worship benefit from this activity. Personal beliefs and/or participation in church services are part of well-balanced living. Each recovering alcoholic needs to review his or her spiritual development and, if necessary, improve the quality and/or quantity of his or her spiritual development.

What is good about your current spiritual development? Write out your answers.

Do you have specific times set aside for spiritual activities?

Are you happy with your spiritual life?

Do you share your spiritual life with others?

What is bad about your spiritual development?

How can you improve your spiritual development?

Make a plan for better spiritual development. Write it down. Make sure the plan is well-balanced and satisfies your spiritual needs. Specify in your plan the steps you will take to improve your spiritual life.

8) Family

As you know, the more time you spent drinking the less time you had for other activities. Many recovering alcoholics experience guilt feelings related to their drinking behavior when around the family. Put these feelings aside. There is nothing you can do to change the past. Now that you are sober, you can have an active, healthy and happy relationship with your family.

What is currently good about your relationship with your family? Write your answers.

Do you spend two to four hours a day with your family?
Are you comfortable around your family?
Do you get along with family members?
What is currently bad about your family situation?
How can you improve your family situation?

Make a plan for better family happiness. Make sure the plan is well-balanced. Is there sufficient time for each family member and for different activities? In your plan, identify the aspect of your family life which you are trying to improve. Write down the plan and list the steps you intend to take to improve your family life.

9) Friends

Friends are a source of comfort and support. They provide both company and opportunities for recreation. Friends with whom we used to drink, who are still drinking, need to be avoided. We need to develop friendships with people who don't drink. One of the easiest ways to return to drinking is to associate with friends who drink.

In what way are your current friends good for you? Write your answers.

Do you need to develop new friends?
Do you have friends who don't drink?
Are you happy with your non-drinking friends?
Do you engage in a variety of recreational activities with your friends?
What about your current friends is detrimental to you?
How can you improve your friendships?

Make a plan for better friendships. Try to develop a variety of friends that are non-drinkers. Pick people with whom you can participate in a number of different activities. When looking for friends, think about what you have to offer. Are you a good friend? In your plan identify the aspects of your friendship you are trying to improve. Write down your plan and specify the steps you are taking to improve the quality and quantity of your friendships.

10) Chores

Chores are always there and never completely finished.

If you are going to live a healthy, sober, mature life, you will need to do your chores.

Make a list of your daily chores, weekly chores and monthly chores. Write out your list now. Develop a plan to get these done. Keep in mind that nobody likes doing chores, you're no different. But chores have to be done. .

What chores do you routinely get done?

What chores do you let slide and do only when you have to?

What chores do you totally ignore?

How can you improve your ability to do your chores?

Make a plan that will allow you to accomplish your chores when necessary. Be specific. When will you do each chore? How will you monitor yourself to see that the chore is being done? Write the plan down.

Make a list of the ten essential life activities. Review the list given earlier in this chapter. Rank them in order. Put in first place that life activity which is most regular and well-balanced in your life. Put in second place that activity which is next well-balanced. Continue this process to number ten which should be the least well-balanced of the ten actions.

For items eight, nine, and ten in the above list, review your plan of action. Is the plan good enough to bring that area of your life into balance?

Emotional Growth (Lunch)

How do you feel reviewing the ten essential areas of your life so systematically? Does it bother you to set plans for each aspect of your life? If so, why? If not, why not?

How will you deal with these feelings constructively?

Sober Life-Style (Coffee Break)

Which of the plans that you developed are you least likely to carry out? Why? What are you going to do about it?

Action for the Day (Dinner)

I   Attend an A.A. meeting. After the meeting, ask a person you barely know to join you for a cup of coffee. During the coffee break, find out from this person what they derive from A.A. attendance.

II   Share with this person what you derive from A.A. attendance.

III   Practice telling the blunt truth. Review your need to be honest. Call your spouse or a close friend and talk about your progress in being truthful. Be truthful!!

Feelings: Review of the Day (Beverage Break)

I   How are you feeling about yourself today? Use at least five sentences to describe how you are feeling about yourself today.

II   How does this contrast with the way you felt about yourself eight days ago? Take at least five sentences to describe how you felt eight days ago and how this contrasts with what you're feeling about yourself today.

III   Practice feeling good. Sometime during the day, find a quiet place where you can be alone for a few minutes. Put all thoughts out of your mind. Review the good things you have accomplished over the past few days and feel good about them.

Daily Reading (While getting ready for bed)

Old Ways - New Ways

By the phrase "old ways" we refer to those actions and habits that led you to seek treatment. It includes the general life-style of alcohol abuse and whatever else was harmful to yourself and to others. The old ways are frequently hard to define. We have a natural inclination to remember them as better than they were. Sometimes individuals even refer to them as the "good old days."

Recovery from alcoholism requires the development of a way of life that enhances sobriety, a way of life which we call sober living. We have to discover the old ways that led up to and supported our alcoholism—those ways that allowed us to live a life that was self-destructive. Not all that we did was harmful or conducive to alcohol abuse. Much that we did before treatment was productive, healthy and happy. We need to know what the old ways were.

Perhaps the best method of identifying the old ways is to study the Fourth Step. The Fourth Step of A.A. allows us to examine our drinking life and to identify those activities that were harmful to ourselves or others. While remembering the old ways, we do not look only at mistakes, peccadillos, or harmful transgressions. When we look for the old ways, we try to identify core character problems and common habits or activities that are harmful and set us up for drinking.

Another good method of identifying the old ways is to ask significant persons in our lives to share with us the truth about ourselves as they see it. When we do this, there are two cautions to keep in mind. The first point to keep in mind is that if we ask someone to share with us our character defects and personal weaknesses as they see them, we must guard against being defensive and not hearing what they say. If we assume that the person we chose is capable, then we should have the trust and humility to accept their judgment. This does not mean that they are totally correct, but that we should be inclined to accept what they say as having some relevance to us.

The second point to keep in mind when we ask another person for their assessment of us is not to be trapped in specifics and details. Don't make the person "prove" that at 4:00 p.m. on Friday the 13th we forgot to do such and such. The whole purpose of this exercise is to discover those habits and actions that set us up for drinking. If the person is willing to share with us their observations, then we should have the humility to accept what they have to offer. What is the suggestion they are making?

Sometimes what we hear will hurt. Sometimes we'll know ahead of time what we will hear from others. We should rise above these distractions, and keep in mind our goal. If we are going to develop new ways, that is, a life-style which enhances and strengthens our sober living, then we have to know what the old ways were.

The next question arises: What do we do about the old ways after we have identified them? The answer is to develop new ways. It is easier to develop new ways than to worry about getting rid of the old ways. The phrase "new ways" is used to describe activities, habits and attitudes that are conducive to sober living. Alcoholics, when drinking, tend to be involved in every kind of activity less than non-drinkers. Except for two activities. The first is watching T.V. It is a safe assumption that the alcoholic spends a lot of time watching T.V., and that at least some of that T.V. time coincides with drinking. The second activity that alcoholics perform as often as non-drinkers is going drinking with friends. Except for these two activities, the alcoholic is less active than the non-drinker in every area. The alcoholic has fewer hobbies, goes out to dinner less often, participates in fewer recreational activities, shops less, doesn't do the chores as often or go to movies as regularly as the non-drinker. The alcoholic does not engage in any activity with as much frequency or intensity as the non-drinker. So, part of the new ways will be the development of well-balanced habits and activities.

Sober living means more than just giving up the drinking of alcoholic beverages. We don't just stop drinking. We start doing other things. These other things are the new ways. Many people who are recovering from alcoholism believe they have only to stop drinking. It is not as simple as that. In fact, many experts feel that alcoholics who want to define recovery merely as quitting drinking are not looking at their whole problem and are denying other concomitant problems and are resisting change and the development of new ways.

There is a saying around A.A. that goes: "When you sober up you have to change your playmates and change your playgrounds." People that resist finding new non-drinking friends, and different things to do and different places to go, have a good possibility of returning to drinking. Face it, if we don't want to drink, then we won't go around with people who drink or to places where drinking goes on. If we do, we increase the chances that we will return to drinking. If we don't want to drink, then we will develop new ways: activities, habits, and attitudes that strengthen sober living.

When we reviewed the old ways we probably found that they focused around our drinking or were designed to protect our drinking. The old ways probably included things like never being at home, never helping out around the house, lying to our spouse about drinking, picking fights or getting into fights over drinking. Having reviewed the old ways we probably feel that many of them were caused by drinking. Now that the drinking has stopped, many of these old ways will cease or be reduced, but we still need to develop new ways.

When we develop our new ways, we should start with specific activities. There is a need for everyone to engage in activities which they find enjoyable and reinforcing. It will be even better if we can find a hobby that others in the family can participate in. Other activities should include helping out around the house, doing routine chores, and taking care of responsibilities. Some of our activity time should be devoted to recreation and entertainment. Keep in mind that we have less chance of drinking at a movie house than we do at a night club.

Reading Review

In two or three sentences, describe the point of today's reading.

How does today's reading pertain to you? Give at least two examples.

Can you implement in your own personal life something from today's reading?

Write down how you can implement today's reading in your life.

Evening Reflection (When in bed)

Spend your evening reflection thinking about the following biblical quotation:

"Trust in the Lord with all your heart, . . .
In all your ways acknowledge Him,
and He will make straight your paths." Prov. 3:5,6

After a few minutes of meditation, reread Steps Two and Three of Alcoholics Anonymous.

Step Two—"Came to believe that a Power greater than ourselves could restore us to sanity."

Step Three—"Made a decision to turn our will and our lives over to the care of God *as we understood Him.*"

Reaffirm your belief and commitment to these steps.

Day Nine—*I Am An Alcoholic . . .*

Morning Meditation (Upon Rising)

Go for a fifteen minute walk. If the weather is inclement, go to a window and let your mind look out the window and take a walk. During this morning walk, communicate on a personal level with your Higher Power. Relate your hopes and fears to your Higher Power. Express gratitude for being alive and possessing the attributes you have. Be thankful for your sobriety.

Thinking About Yourself (Breakfast)

Sober living is strengthened when the majority of our day is organized. This is not to say that we must schedule *every* minute of our day. That would be overdoing it.

Review the major activities that you need to perform in order to have a happy, orderly, well-balanced life. Check the items which you *will do*. If you will do them more than once a day, write it down. Fill in how many hours each day and each week you will spend in each activity.

	DAILY		**WEEKLY**	
	How many times a day	How many hours a day	How many times a week	How many hours a week
Sleep	_____	_____	_____	_____
Eat	_____	_____	_____	_____
Work	_____	_____	_____	_____
Recreate	_____	_____	_____	_____
Pray	_____	_____	_____	_____
Play	_____	_____	_____	_____
Shower & Bathe	_____	_____	_____	_____
Watch T.V.	_____	_____	_____	_____
Exercise	_____	_____	_____	_____
Talk to Family	_____	_____	_____	_____
Drive	_____	_____	_____	_____
Shop	_____	_____	_____	_____
Volunteer Work	_____	_____	_____	_____
A.A. meetings	_____	_____	_____	_____

Church	_____	_____	_____	_____
Chores	_____	_____	_____	_____
Make Bed	_____	_____	_____	_____
Food Shopping	_____	_____	_____	_____
Clean House	_____	_____	_____	_____
Laundry	_____	_____	_____	_____
Read	_____	_____	_____	_____
Visit	_____	_____	_____	_____
Go to Movies	_____	_____	_____	_____
Mow Lawn and other Yard Chores	_____	_____	_____	_____
Rest	_____	_____	_____	_____
Doing Nothing	_____	_____	_____	_____
Other Activities	_____	_____	_____	_____

The purpose of the exercise above is to see how you spend your week. There are 168 hours in a week. You are trying to examine whether or not you get done what you want to do during the week. Are you satisfied that you have distributed your time in a way which allows for well-balanced living?

There are four categories of healthy living, biological, social, productive and spiritual. From the list above, make an estimate of the total time you devote to each area.

Biological	Weekly Total Hours	**Social**	Weekly Total Hours
Sleep	_____	Family Time	_____
Eat	_____	Visiting	_____
Bathroom	_____	Recreating	_____
Exercise	_____		
Ideal 70 hours a week		Ideal 21 hours a week	
My total	_____	My total	_____

Productive	Weekly Total Hours	**Spiritual**	Weekly Total Hours
Work	_____	Church	_____
Chores	_____	A.A.	_____
Shopping	_____	Prayer	_____
Cleaning	_____	Reading	_____
Laundry	_____	Volunteering	_____
Ideal 60 hours a week		Ideal 15 hours a week	
My total _____		My total _____	

Emotional Growth (Lunch)

When we were children, an adult figure, usually a parent or teacher, organized our day. They made sure we did what we had to do when we had to do it and in the way we had to do it. Usually, during adolescence, we begin organizing our own lives and taking care of ourselves. During adolescence we often feel resentment when an adult figure tells us what to do or tries to organize our lives. This is a part of growing up.

Recovery from alcoholism is similar. Others give us advice or try to organize our lives. We may feel resentment, anger or some other negative emotion. Filling out a sober living schedule can cause a similar emotional reaction. There is a tendency to feel this is childish, immature and unnecessary. Often, there are impulses to gloss over this schedule, to view the activity as beneath us or even forget to do it. These are dangerous feelings. This schedule will help you to develop new ways of living. Failing to plan out your new ways increases your chances of returning to the old ways.

Sober living is well-balanced living. It is also disciplined living. Discipline yourself to establish a sober living schedule.

How do you feel about developing a sober living schedule? Write out your answers.

Do you think that your feeling will get in the way of following your sober living schedule? If so, how? What are you going to do about it? If not, why not?

How will you deal with future negative emotions that might arise from following the sober living schedule? Be specific. Develop a plan of action.

Sober Life-Style (Coffee Break)

Most alcoholics, when they were drinking, spent too many hours doing some things (drinking) and not enough hours doing other things. Well-balanced living does not mean minute to minute scheduling. It does mean that we do enough of all that we need to do for healthy living; but not too much of any one thing.

Make a rough schedule of how you intend to allot your time and your activities. Be as specific as you can, but remember the purpose of scheduling is to organize your time into well-balanced, happy, sober living.

On the next page is an example of a sober living schedule. The purpose of the sober living schedule is to help you organize your life. Don't feel overwhelmed by the task. The purpose is not to tie you down, but rather to help you see that you have time to include all the essential activities of well-balanced living.

Review the sample sober living schedule. In your notebook, write out your own sober living schedule.

Sober Living Schedule

	Saturday	Sunday	Monday	Tuesday	Wednesday	Thursday	Friday
6:00 a.m.	Rise	Rise-meditate	Rise-meditate	Rise-meditate	Rise-meditate	Rise-meditate	Rise-meditate
7:00 a.m.	Meditate	Groom	Groom	Groom	Groom	Groom	Groom
8:00 a.m.	Groom	Church	Breakfast	Breakfast	Breakfast	Breakfast	Breakfast
9:00 a.m.	Breakfast	Breakfast	Reading	Reading	Reading	Reading	Reading
10:00 a.m.	House chores	Family time	Work	Work	Work	Work	Work
11:00 a.m.	Lunch	Lunch					
12:00 p.m.			Lunch	Lunch	Lunch	Lunch	Lunch
1:00 p.m.							
2:00 p.m.	Shopping	Outside recreation or yard work	Walk	Walk	Walk	Walk	Walk
3:00 p.m.	Outside recreation						
4:00 p.m.							
5:00 p.m.	Read paper	Read paper	Read paper	Read paper	Read paper	Read paper	Read paper
6:00 p.m.	Dinner	Dinner	Dinner	Dinner	Dinner	Dinner	Dinner
7:00 p.m.							
8:00 p.m.	AA meeting	Visit mother in nursing home	Tidy up house AA meeting	T.V.	T.V.	AA meeting	Movie or dancing
9:00 p.m.							
10:00 p.m.							
11:00 p.m.	Reflection	Reflection	Reflection	Reflection	Reflection	Reflection	Reflection
12:00 a.m.	Bed	Bed	Bed	Bed	Bed	Bed	Bed
1:00 a.m.							
2:00 a.m.							
3:00 a.m.							
4:00 a.m.							
5:00 a.m.							

MORNING · AFTERNOON · EVENING · NIGHT

<u>Sober Living Schedule Questionnaire</u>

Answer each item with a "yes" or a "no."

	Yes	No
1. Are you comfortable with your sober living schedule?	____	____
2. Is there a sufficient number of A.A. meetings built into it?	____	____
3. Do you think you have planned enough time to be with your family?	____	____
4. Do you think you have planned enough spiritual time?	____	____
5. If you unconsciously were looking for a time to sneak a few drinks, is your sober living schedule so sound and well-balanced that it would be almost impossible to sneak in a few drinks?	____	____
6. Did you plan enough time to be by yourself for thinking and relaxing?	____	____
7. Do you think you will follow your sober living schedule fairly closely?	____	____
8. Would you be willing to show your sober living schedule to your spouse or employer?	____	____
9. Will the sober living schedule help you stay sober?	____	____
10. Is your sober living schedule so well-planned and thought-out that it would be hard to improve?	____	____

If you answered three or more of the above ten questions "no," then you have to go back and redevelop your sober living plan. Seek some help from your spouse or close sober friend.

Action for the Day (Dinner)

I   Begin to look for an A.A. sponsor. The A.A. sponsor is an important step for sober living. The sponsor should be a mature, stable person who has a good length of sober living already. The sponsor should live as he talks. Try to find someone who faithfully lives and practices the Twelve

Steps and Traditions of A.A., someone who will be willing to share with you and assist you to develop a sound A.A. way of life.

II   Jot down three or four names of people you think are likely candidates to be your sponsor. Use only the first name and the last initial. Write in your notebook.

III   Find three reasons why you think each person is a possible candidate. Write out three reasons for each candidate.

IV   Go to an A.A. meeting. Before or after the meeting, talk to some of the A.A. old-timers about the value of a sponsor.

Feelings: Review of the Day (Beverage Break)

I   How do you feel about finding a sponsor? Write your answers in your notebook.

II   How do you think having a sponsor will make you feel? Take at least five sentences to describe your feelings about having a sponsor.

III   Share these feelings about having a sponsor with another person.

IV   Tonight when you go to bed, practice relaxation before falling asleep. Lay flat on your back. Systematically practice getting relaxed. First tighten the muscles in your feet. Then relax them. Notice the difference between the tense feeling when you tighten the muscles and the relaxed feeling when you let go. After your feet, practice this same exercise with your legs, your stomach, your chest, your hands, your arms and your shoulders. Finally, tighten and relax your neck and then your head and face. First tighten the muscles and then say, "relax," and let the muscles go. Practice this tonight. After you relax each set of muscles, enjoy the feeling. After you've relaxed your whole body, lie quietly. RELAX.

Daily Reading (While getting ready for bed)

Thinking, Feeling and Doing
(Thinking)

Many people go through life without giving much attention to how their thoughts and feelings affect their actions. Some people don't even recognize that there is a distinction between thoughts and feelings. It is true that some experiences arouse both thoughts and feelings. Yet certain situations create definite thoughts or specific feelings. Being able to identify our thoughts and our thinking style allows us to deal clearly and precisely with the problem we face. Being able to recognize and deal with feelings effectively allows us to understand what is going on inside us, and enables us to better face up to situations confronting us.

Thinking is considered by many to be a form of sub-vocal speech. It is like talking to ourselves. Thinking is both deliberate and incidental. We can deliberately decide to "think about" what we will have for dinner tonight. Thinking can also be either incidental or reactive. If, for example, while driving the car, we see a red sign with four letters in white printed on it, we automatically begin to put a foot on the brake to bring the car to a stop. We will not focus here on incidental or reactive thinking. This skill is inherent, and so long as we eat, exercise and rest properly, it will function relatively stably throughout most of our lives.

Deliberate thinking has a good deal of control over us. Likewise, we can control our thinking. The thinking process usually starts with something specific that happens in our lives. For example, the alarm fails to go off in the morning and we wake up an hour late. This is the specific stimulus which signals the thinking to begin. Some people do no thinking at all, and immediately panic: "Oh, I'm going to be late for work— I'll be fired!" These people tend to get nervous and think the same thoughts over and over again: "I'm going to be late—I'll be fired." In this instance repetitive thinking is getting in the way of clear and deliberate action. It is also arousing nervous feelings which make problem-solving all the more difficult. Uncontrolled thought, such as repetitive thinking, can be problem-creating rather than problem-solving.

Another person whose alarm did not go off and who overslept by an hour might immediately recognize that he or she will be late for work. This recognition triggers problem-solving thinking and action: "I'm late, what do I need to do? Well, I better call the boss and say I overslept, I'll be there as soon as I can. Next, as quickly as possible, I will get cleaned up and dressed. I'll skip breakfast so I can get to work more quickly." This person then puts these thoughts into action.

Looks easy doesn't it? Well, it's not always easy, but it is possible. If thinking is to be successful, it has to follow a plan. First, what is the purpose of the thinking? What goal are we setting? Where do we have to go to find the answer? Do we have to consult someone? Get advice from someone? Look up the answer in a book? In other words, thinking is not just mulling thoughts over and over in our heads. Thinking is specific mental work. It is mental problem-solving. It is the mental steps that we take before we put a plan of action into effect. It is developing a mental plan of action to solve problems or take care of things that need to be done. Without sound planning (thinking), our actions will be haphazard and random.

Purposeful thinking enables us to achieve success in life by helping us solve problems as they arise, helping us set goals in our lives and helping us understand things that happen to us. Recovering alcoholics frequently have problems with purposeful thinking. These problems are due to the influence drinking had on our thinking process. When a person is drinking, the alcohol, and the desire for alcohol, warp the thinking process. Individuals who have never lied, learn to lie like troopers and cover up their alcoholism. People who were objective and realistic in their thinking become biased, closed-minded, and opinionated when they become alcoholic.

Recovering alcoholics sometimes carry over faulty thinking habits from their drinking days. These faulty thinking habits are dangerous and can encourage the recovering alcoholic to return to drinking. Some of the common faulty thinking habits that recovering alcoholics should watch for are:

Bias—having an answer or having *the* answer for almost everything. This goes along with being closed-minded, narrow-minded and prejudiced. This kind of faulty thinking habit keeps an individual in a small self-contained world. You see many people like this in the world. You see many people like this even in A.A. They have the answer. They are rigid and tend to be orthodox, they religiously follow the "rules." These people get angry when newcomers or others offer suggestions or try to change things. Closed-minded thinkers slavishly try to keep their world ordered. They also try to be in charge. They want everything checked out and approved by them. These narrow-minded, opinionated, rigid people are unhappy and defensive. They force their thinking into pigeon holes. There is no room for change and there is definitely no room for another person's opinion.

Obsession—going over and over the same thoughts. Sometimes this style of repetitive thinking is accompanied by repetitive actions. People who keep grudges, or gather resentments, or harbor grievances, are going over and over the same thoughts. These people are busy thinking about incidents and situations that are past. They are thinking of ways to get even with someone they think slighted them. They are continuously thinking of ways to make themselves look good. They pay constant attention to setting the world straight.

Another type of obsession is constantly thinking about every ache and pain in the body, constantly waiting for something to go wrong. People with this obsession are apprehensive thinkers. Something is going to happen, so they will worry about it. Over and over they think of all the possible things that could go wrong. They are worriers, and worry is repetitive thinking.

Obsessive, repetitive thinking is faulty thinking. It is destructive of problem-solving. It is time-consuming. Energy is spent doing the same thing over and over.

Depression—always being down in the dumps emotionally.

This includes people who see only problems. They are prophets of doom and gloom. When you talk to this kind of person, nothing is right. Something is always wrong or going to be wrong. Depressive thinkers find all the reasons why they will fail and use them as excuses to avoid trying. This type of faulty thinking suggests, "Why bother to try, I'm going to fail anyway."

Euphoria—being very high emotionally. This is the person who is always happy. Nothing is ever wrong. This person usually smiles constantly, always sees "the brighter side," is a "goody two-shoes."

How do you review your thinking so that you know that it is healthy, efficient and problem-solving? This is hard to do, especially since many people are convinced that they are right. They reinforce their opinions and actions with thought.

The first step in assessing the quality of your thinking is to check it out with other people. Try to choose people who, in your opinion, are mature, successful and responsible. Share a personal thought with them and listen to their opinion. If you get concurrence, good! If you continue to get disagreement, you may seriously think about changing your thoughts and opinions.

Reading Review

In two or three sentences, describe the point of today's reading.

How does today's reading pertain to you? Give at least two examples.

Can you implement in your personal life something from today's reading? Write down how you can implement today's reading in your life.

Evening Reflection (When in bed)

Tonight contemplate your need to help. Think about your recovery from alcoholism and all the people who have been instrumental in your decision to seek treatment and recovery. Feel gratitude toward those who have helped you. Finally, think of the many ways you continue to need help. Mentally, make a note of the help your A.A. sponsor can give you.

Day Ten—*I Am Responsible*

Morning Meditation (Upon Rising)

Meditate on the concepts of self-discipline. Think of areas in your life in which self-discipline plays an important role. Contemplate nature, looking for order and discipline. Are you in control of your life as much as you would like to be? Do you need to develop and practice self-discipline?

Thinking About Yourself (Breakfast)

For the past ten days you have worked in this book. So far, you have focused on a commitment to Step One—"We admitted we were powerless over alcohol—that our lives had become unmanageable."

You have had a spiritual awakening. You have studied and come to grips with Steps Two and Three of Alcoholics Anonymous. Step Two—"Came to believe that a Power greater than ourselves could restore us to sanity." Step Three—"Made a decision to turn our will and our lives over to the care of God *as we understood Him.*" You intend to avoid drinking by developing sober living.

Sober living is a well-balanced, orderly, organized life. People who return to drinking usually do so because they tried to pick up their lives where they left off before treatment. They continue to do things in the same way they did before they stopped drinking. But now they try to do it without drinking.

This will not work. Sobriety is not enough; you need to practice your sober living plan.

List in your notebook ten reasons why you might not follow your sober living plan and/or reasons why you would stop practicing your sober living plan.

Which two of the above ten reasons are the most likely reasons you would stop following your sober living plan? Write them down.

Self-discipline is the only way you will practice sober living daily. You may learn all the reasons why you drank excessively; you may know all the things necessary for sober living and you may really want sober living; but unless you have the self-discipline to practice sober living, you will return to drinking.

What is self-discipline? It is the ability to do what you need to do when you need to do it. People with poor self-discipline deceive themselves. They give themselves all kinds of excuses to do whatever they want. They talk themselves into believing that a lie is the truth. They use excuses, rationalizations, shortcuts, everything but the truth. All kinds of reasons but the truth. The truth is this: sober living is good for you.

Many alcoholics prepare themselves for failure by finding reasons why they can't perfectly complete their sober living plan. This is self-deceit. It is better to complete 80% of your sober living plan for the day than to drink. You are not God. You can't do anything perfectly so don't evade your sober living plan by a lie.

Self-discipline is the ability to put into action your sober living plan. Do this by getting into the habit of following your plan. Establish definite patterns, and then follow them. If you want to make sure that you will accomplish your sober living plan each day, start off each day with a morning meditation. During these 10 or 15 minutes, review your purpose in life. Remind yourself that sober living is good for you. Then make plans and set goals for that day. At the end of the day spend 10 or 15 minutes in reflection. Examine the way you spent the day. Put yourself in touch with your world.

These two practices (a morning meditation and an evening reflection) can be the basis for your self-discipline.

List ten counter-measures you can take to insure that you will follow the sober living plan. Look at each of the ten reasons you gave for not following your sober living plan, and develop an antidote for each one. Write it out.

We have learned that people who practice their sober living plan faithfully, until it becomes a way of life, do so by sharing the plan with others. Following your plan in isolation leaves the responsibility totally on you. Following your plan with the help of another person shares the responsibility. Review the plan and see how many people are routinely included in the plan.

Make a list of the people in your plan. There should be at least three.

Share your sober living plan with three people. Try to choose individuals who fit into one of the following categories:

a) Spouse
b) Best friend (non-drinker)
c) Parent
d) Job supervisor, or employer
e) A.A. sponsor
f) Brother or sister

The three people you choose should be mature, stable people who are non-drinkers; or at least individuals who do not have a drinking problem and will be willing not to drink in your presence.

The role of the person with whom you share your sober living plan is to meet with you or talk to you on the phone at least once a week. In this conversation, you should review your weekly progress.

This may be difficult for you. Your pride may get in the way. You may feel like a child. DO IT. See these people or call them, but share with three people your sober living plan. Eat your pride. If you want to practice sober living successfully, you need all the help you can get.

Emotional Growth (Lunch)

Step Four of Alcoholics Anonymous reads—"Made a searching and fearless moral inventory of ourselves."

What do you think is the purpose of the Fourth Step of A.A.? What does the Fourth Step have to do with your recovery from alcoholism? Be detailed and specific in your answer. Write out your answer.

How do you feel about examining yourself and your actions by taking a searching and fearless moral inventory?

Step Five goes even further. It reads, "Admitted to God, to ourselves, and to another human being the exact nature of our wrongs." What do you think is the purpose of the Fifth Step? What does the Fifth Step have to do with your recovery from alcoholism? Be specific in your answer.

How do you feel about the idea of taking a Fifth Step?

Reread Steps Four and Five of A.A. Think about these steps. How does the completion of these steps relate to your own recovery? When the time comes in the next couple of days to take your Fourth and Fifth Steps, how will you deal with the feelings mentioned above?

At the next A.A. meeting you attend discuss the Fourth and Fifth Steps with an A.A. member you admire. Find out how they dealt with their emotions when making these two steps.

Sober Life-Style (Coffee Break)

Recovery from alcoholism requires a period of dependency. As we learn about ourselves; about how to solve problems and how to live our A.A. program, we need help. Your A.A. sponsor is an excellent source of support and assistance, especially in the early stages of recovery.

You have already given considerable thought about an A.A. sponsor. You have made a list of three people whom you think would be good initial A.A. sponsors for you. You have talked to a number of A.A. people about the role of sponsorship in recovery, as well as how to get a sponsor.

Following are some tips in getting and using an A.A. sponsor:

1) Make a list of two or three people you think would make good A.A. sponsors for you.

2) Study each one closely. Do they live a good A.A. program? Do they have an established period of stable, sober living?

3) Decide how you intend to work with your sponsor. Do you intend to meet regularly? Do you intend to meet casually? Will there be a definite review and discussion of your A.A. program? Be specific and detailed in what you think you need from an A.A. sponsor.

4) Choose one of the possible A.A. sponsors from your list. Talk to that person. See if they would be willing to be your A.A. sponsor. Discuss with them how they view their role of sponsorship. Agree to the specifics of your relation-

ship. When will you meet? Where will you meet?

5) If you are both willing, begin your relationship with your new sponsor. If both of you are not willing, try the next person on your list. Keep going until you have a sponsor.

Action for the Day (Dinner)

I   Write a letter to one of the people with whom you verbally shared your sober living plan. In that letter include:

   a) Why you need a sober living plan.

   b) Why you need their help with it.

   c) What you would want them to do.

   d) Enclose a copy of your sober living plan.

II Attend an A.A. meeting.

III Get an A.A. sponsor for yourself.

Feelings: Review of the Day (Beverage Break)

I   How do you feel about asking someone to help with your sober living plan? Use at least five sentences to describe this feeling.

II Do you feel the people you listed will help you practice sober living? Be specific. How will they help? How will they not help? How do you know the difference?

III Yesterday, for the first time, you practiced relaxation. This exercise is a very important step in the development of sober living. Many alcoholics drink when they are up-tight, nervous, or anxious. They do not know how to relax. The ability to relax is essential for healthy living. Animals have the ability to turn off their anxiety. For example, the rabbit which successfully avoids a fox during the chase by finding a safe haven, can immediately "turn off" its nervousness. People have difficulty turning off anxiety, but it is not impossible. You can learn to do this.

Relaxation exercises are designed to teach you how to turn off your anxieties by relaxing. It is impossible to be nervous and relaxed at the same time. If you are nervous and you make yourself relax, you are no longer nervous.

1) Tighten your right foot—relax it. Notice how the foot feels

when relaxed.

2) Tighten your left foot—relax it. Notice how the foot feels when relaxed.

3) Tighten your right leg—relax it. Notice how the leg feels when relaxed.

4) Tighten your left leg—relax it. Notice how the leg feels when relaxed.

5) Tighten your stomach—relax it. Notice how the stomach feels when relaxed.

6) Tighten your right hand—relax it. Notice how the hand feels when relaxed.

7) Tighten your left hand—relax it. Notice how the hand feels when relaxed.

8) Tighten your right arm—relax it. Notice how the arm feels when relaxed.

9) Tighten your left arm—relax it. Notice how the arm feels when relaxed.

10) Tighten your shoulders—relax them. Notice how they feel when relaxed.

11) Tighten your neck and face muscles—relax them. Notice how they feel when relaxed.

12) Lie quietly. Take a deep breath and hold it. Exhale. Say to yourself three times: Relax, Relax, Relax.

Daily Reading (While getting ready for bed)

Thinking, Feeling and Doing
(Feeling)

American culture has inadequate allowances for feelings. Everyone has feelings, yet in American culture, we receive confusing messages about feelings. For example: "If you feel good say so, but don't say anything if you feel bad." Men are told, "It is not manly to express your feelings, feelings are feminine." Most of these messages are designed to control or repress feelings. They are designed for the comfort of those around us. These emotional controls allow everybody to pretend everything is fine. They keep relationships safe and shallow. Our culture is afraid of emotional expression and encourages people to remain safe and avoid intimacy and sharing. This is an immature and naive cultural attitude.

On the other hand, during the past decade or so in America, there has been an overreaction to our emotional guardedness. This emotional overreaction lets it all hang out. This flippant, shallow approach encourages us to wear our emotions on our shirt sleeves. Cute buttons and catchy sayings are bandied about as if they were genuine expressions of emotion, rather than the mere symbols of emotion which they actually are.

Nevertheless, the emotional growth of the past ten years is of some value. Such a movement was necessary because of the oppressive restraint on emotion that existed in American culture. Now it is time for us to find a middle ground between repression and over-expression.

In general, every recovering alcoholic needs to develop an ability to express and receive emotion. Alcoholism, a progressive, self-destructive illness, is also a selfish and self-centered habit. Alcohol is a demanding mistress or lover. The more time you spend with alcohol, the more alcohol demands of you. Finally, for many, it becomes an exclusive relationship between the alcoholic and the alcohol.

What is healthy expression and reception of feelings? The best way to answer this question is to point out the two most common problems that recovering alcoholics have with feelings. The first problem is the repression of feelings. The second problem is sensitizing.

People who repress their feelings or who refuse to receive the expression of feeling from others are common. This is especially common among American males. This problem is the product of a culture in which individuals learn that it is safest to keep feelings deep down inside. They tend to be task-oriented, that is, they are more inclined to get the job done than to experience feelings about how the job affects those around them. Represser type alcoholics keep all their feelings locked inside themselves. Male recovering alcoholics are often afraid that if they express tenderness or warmth they will lose control and maybe even cry. They believe they have to hold down their feelings because if they show anger, they're likely to lose control of their tempers.

People who repress their feelings do so to avoid losing control. They think that if they express their feelings they may show weakness or ugliness. So they prefer to be controlled and unemotional. This creates problems for recovering alcoholics. Such repression continues to isolate the recovering alcoholic from closeness with others. This is an unnatural situation because the represser knows that he has feelings yet doesn't know how to express them for fear of losing control.

Sensitizers, on the other hand, are individuals who dwell on their feelngs. These recovering alcoholics spend a lot of time telling anyone who will listen exactly how they feel about almost everything. They overreact to their feelings. They wear down everyone around them. They look for instant intimacy. They are surprised and hurt if they don't find it. These people frequently live on an emotional roller coaster. Repressers tend to isolate themselves from emotional sharing with others. Sensitizers tend to dump their most intense and personal feelings on anyone who will listen.

The represser emotionally isolates himself, the sensitizer emotionally squanders himself. Healthy emotional living is neither condition. Healthy, well-balanced sober living is the ability to express our feelings openly and honestly to individuals who share some degree of personal closeness with us. The recovering alcoholic needs to determine whether he is more of a represser or a sensitizer. Once you identify your emotional style, you can begin to develop healthier ways of sharing and receiving feelings. If you tend to be a represser, you need to develop the ability to express and receive feelings without discomfort. If you tend to be a sensitizer, you have to work on less demanding forms of emotional exchange.

In general, it is good for sensitizers to engage in some organized form of emotional development. Usually this kind of training and experience is available at local mental health centers. There are many emotional growth programs, and not all of them are good. Always check the credentials of any emotional growth counselors. Ask to see a diploma and certificate. Beware of charlatans.

How do feelings work in our lives? Essentially, feelings are interior bodily reactions to situations and events around us. For example, if something sad happens to us, we feel down, blue and depressed. We have a heavy, dull feeling inside. We don't feel like doing anything. Our sleep is interrupted, or we don't feel like eating. Feelings are very physical reactions to whatever happens to us.

Feelings are neither good nor bad. They are only reactions to what happens to us. What we do with our feelings is the important thing. We can do something about how we handle feelings. Having the feeling is a reaction. Handling the feeling is a choice.

Since feelings are physical they affect us physically. They can drain energy when we feel depressed or sad. They can generate energy when we feel excited or euphoric. Feelings can be intimate when we feel warm and close to another person. Feelings can be social when we feel comradery with the group. Feelings can hurt or feel good. We can feel lonely or sociable. There's a feeling for every occasion.

How can we better handle our feelings? There is no single or simple answer to this question. The best answer is that handling feelings requires a well-balanced approach. That is, we neither underreact nor overreact to our feelings. We neither keep feelings entirely to ourselves nor show every feeling we have.

Emotional health rests on the ability to recognize our feelings. When something happens to you, take time to process your reaction. What are you feeling? Put a label on the experience: "I feel happy, I feel sad, I feel sexy." After you label the feeling and recognize that you have the feeling, determine if it is a personal, intimate feeling or if it is a feeling that you would like to share with another person. Share the appropriate feelings with people who are close to you. Keep personal feelings to yourself. How do you know the difference? By knowing if you tend to be a represser or a sensitizer. If you tend to be a represser, you need to encourage yourself to share your feelings more. If you are a sensitizer, you need to practice keeping your feelings more in check.

Finally, if feelings continue to be a problem for you when you practice sober living, go to a mental health center and get some help in this area.

Reading Review

In two or three sentences, describe the point of today's reading.

How does today's reading pertain to you? Give at least two examples.

Can you implement in your life something from today's reading? Write down how you can implement today's reading in your life.

Evening Reflection (When in bed)

Review your sober living plan. Feel a sense of well-being that your life is beginning to come together. Feel gratitude to your Higher Power for the good that is happening to you. Express that gratitude to your Higher Power.

Day Eleven—*I Have Told The Truth*

Morning Meditation (Upon Rising)

Contemplate truth this morning. Keep your thoughts simple. What is truth? What is the role of truth in your sober living? Spend time thinking about how you know the truth and especially on the thought, "How do I live the truth?"

Thinking About Yourself (Breakfast)

A few days ago we talked about truth. We discovered that alcoholism was built upon self-deception. We concluded by developing a plan for telling the truth.

What are your three most common ways of distorting the truth? Write out your answers.

Have you told any lies, direct or indirect, on purpose or accidental, large or small, since you developed a plan of action for honesty? Let's review common ways of lying that the alcoholic uses. If you have used one of the following lies don't just put down "yes." Write down the entire incident in your notebook.

1) Minimizing—reduced the truth. Have you minimized anything lately? If so, what? Be specific. Write out your answers.
2) Outright denial—told a direct lie. Have you actually told a direct lie? If so, put it down.
3) Hostility—gotten mad so you wouldn't have to face up to something. Have you used hostility to avoid the truth? Be specific.
4) Diversion—changed the topic to avoid the truth. Put down a specific example if you used this technique lately.
5) Blaming—accused someone or something for a problem you might have. Put down the specific example if you used this technique to avoid the truth.
6) Rationalizing—made an excuse for a problem that you've had lately. Put it down.
7) Intellectualized—used lots of words to explain away a problem. Jot it down if you have used this technique.

8) Exaggeration—increased something, or made it better than it was. Have you made yourself appear better than you are?

9) Alibis—made up excuses for personal shortcomings, or for someone else's shortcomings. Have you used an alibi? Write it out.

What kind of truth is the hardest for you to tell? What types of lying are you inclined to use?

Write a story entitled: *How I Had Problems Telling The Truth And What I Did About It.*

Emotional Growth (Lunch)

Step Four of Alcoholics Anonymous states—"Made a searching and fearless moral inventory of ourselves." Step Five continues—"Admitted to God, to ourselves, and to another human being the exact nature of our wrongs." These two steps are an exercise in the truth.

Many people fear the truth. They are more comfortable with their little self-deceptions. They feel discomfort at the thought of life without little exaggerations or little denials. This is a very natural and ordinary reaction. For many people these little lies have been repeated so many times they seem like the truth. The truth can seem foreign and unappealing. How do we live the truth? How do we find a sense of well-being with the truth?

In order to answer these questions, an individual needs first to find out the truth about himself or herself. The truth sees both sides of any issue. The truth is both our good side and our bad side. The truth is our struggle to live each day. What is your truth? Who are you? You will find a truth guide below. It is an opportunity for you to see yourself honestly.

Truth Guide

Describe yourself in general; your body, your soul and your mind. Write out your answers.

What do you look like? Describe your good physical attributes as well as those physical attributes you don't like.

What are your talents?
What are your weaknesses?
What do people like about you?
What do people dislike about you?
What do you like about yourself?
What do you dislike about yourself?
Write a paragraph entitled *The Truth About Me.*

Sober Life-Style (Coffee Break)

A few days ago you developed an honesty plan. Write down that honesty plan again.

Have you been making an effort every day to live the truth by telling the blunt truth? If so, how do you remind yourself to do this? If not, why not?

Is there a special time each day when you review the quality of the truth in your life? Do you think this could be part of your evening meditation? How do you plan to remind yourself to practice telling the truth to yourself at all times?

Action for the Day (Dinner)

I   Call someone who knows that you are in a treatment program. Tell this person how you have either succeeded or failed in telling the truth. Point out your successes as well as your lies. Be blunt and honest with this person.

II Attend an A.A. meeting. At this meeting, if you have the opportunity, talk about honesty and its role in sober living.

III After the A.A. meeting, talk to someone. Find out from that person how lying played a role in their drinking and how honesty is part of their sober living.

Feelings: Review of the Day (Beverage Break)

I   How do you feel about all this emphasis on truth telling? Write your answers in your notebook.

II Are you using denial as a way to avoid seeing your lies? Explain your answer.

III Practice feeling good. What do you have to do or think to feel good? Do it.

IV   Tonight before going to sleep, practice your relaxation exercises. Lie in bed quietly. First take your right hand and tighten it. Next relax it. Let it smooth out. Be comfortable and relaxed. The purpose of the exercise is to understand what a tight tense feeling is, and then to practice letting that tense feeling relax. Practice tensing and then relaxing the following muscles: Right hand, right forearm, right bicep, left hand, left forearm, left bicep, right foot, right calf, right thigh, left foot, left calf, left thigh, stomach, chest, shoulders, neck, face, forehead, scalp.

First tense the muscle. Hold it tense for three seconds. Then relax the muscle. Let it smooth out for ten seconds. Say to yourself, "relax." Wait ten seconds and then proceed to the next muscle.

After you have successfully tensed and relaxed these muscles, enjoy the relaxed feeling. Concentrate for one minute on this relaxed state.

Daily Reading (While getting ready for bed)

Thinking, Feeling and Doing
(Doing)

Most of us do not plan our actions. Instead, we react to situations as they arise. Little planning goes into our actions and things just happen to us.

A life-style where much of the action just happens, leaves the individual at the mercy of his reactions. Most action should be the logical and emotionally consistent outcome of thinking and feeling. It is difficult to talk about thinking and feeling before we act without seeming to suggest that people should become robots. That is not the intention of this reading. The purpose of this reading is to suggest that, for the recovering alcoholic, it is good for actions to be preceded by and followed up by thought and feeling reviews.

"Doing what comes naturally" is the catchy lyric of a popular show tune. However, for the recovering alcoholic, doing what comes naturally results in self-destruction. This is an important point to make. Alcoholism is a form of self-destruction. By the time the alcoholic chooses to do something about his drinking, he is well along the road to self-destruction. Doing what comes naturally means a return to drinking and a continuation of the self-destructive process.

How does a recovering alcoholic remain natural, spontaneous and happy, and yet avoid doing those things that are harmful? It requires the coordination of action with thoughts and feelings. Doing what comes naturally implies that there is little thought and emotion involved with action. However, successful living is the ability to act upon thoughts and feelings. Successful living requires planning. Planning does not do away with spontaneity, planning limits spontaneity to a range of preplanned options.

Action is the best way to develop a happy life. People who are depressed tend to sit around a lot. People who are nervous spend a lot of time thinking about what to do. People who are drinking spend a lot of time drinking. People who participate in activities have less time to worry, feel depressed or drink. Activity is not the cure-all for life's problems, but it is a good place to start.

Look at your day. Is it well-balanced? Do you work forty hours a week? Do you have a hobby? Do you recreate daily? Do you exercise? Do you visit friends or go shopping? Do you do chores? Most people could better organize their lives. Look at how you spend your day. Are there ways you can reorganize your day to become involved in more activities? If so, do it.

A final word needs to be said about action. There will be no action without self-discipline. People with problems, especially people with drinking problems, can think of many ways to solve their problems. Frequently, their ideas require healthy action. The only problem is, they don't do it.

Self-discipline means doing what you have to do when you have to do it. The use of morning meditation to plan your day and evening reflection to review your day is a good way to monitor your actions. It's a good way to establish self-discipline.

Doing what you have to do, because you have decided to do it, is the cornerstone of responsible living and the foundation of happiness. You won't always be happy if you do what you have to do, but if you establish a well-balanced sober living plan and do it, come rain or shine, you will be happier than you used to be. That's progress, isn't it?

Reading Review

In two or three sentences, describe the point of today's reading.

How does today's reading pertain to you? Give at least two examples.

Can you implement in your life something from today's reading? Write down how you can implement today's reading in your life.

Evening Reflection (When in bed)

Close the day with a prayer of gratitude. Be thankful for all the good in your life. Think of all the facets of your life that are good. Express gratitude to your Higher Power. Plan to express gratitude to all those that have helped you achieve your current state of sober living.

Think about the serenity prayer:

"God grant me the Serenity to accept
the things I cannot change,
Courage to change the things I can,
and Wisdom to know the difference."

Day Twelve—God Grant Me the Courage . . .

Morning Meditation (Upon Rising)

Spend this morning contemplating the spiritual virtues of Faith. We cannot control every aspect of life. To some extent our destiny is outside of our control. Faith is the belief in our Higher Power that whatever we cannot control will work out for our well-being. Step Two of A.A. is an act of faith—"Came to believe that a Power greater than ourselves could restore us to sanity."

Faith is the belief that God has a plan for us. This kind of spiritual faith helps us to accept our assets and virtues as well as our problems and character defects. This does not mean that we should stop trying to live life and solve problems. This is faith: to believe that everything depends on God, but to work as if everything depends on us.

This morning in meditation, review your faith in God, your faith in those around you and especially your faith in yourself. Verbally express your faith in God, those around you and yourself during this meditation.

Thinking About Yourself (Breakfast)

Step Four of Alcoholics Anonymous reads—"Made a searching and fearless moral inventory of ourselves." Step Five of A.A. reads—"Admitted to God, to ourselves and to another human being the exact nature of our wrongs."

The purpose of these two steps is to ask for forgiveness and to wipe clean the slate of our wrongdoings. These steps allow us the chance to begin a new, sober life.

There is no such thing as the perfect Fourth or Fifth Step. Keep in mind the purpose of these steps: to identify our mistakes and wrongdoings and to unload them on God and another person.

Many people miss the point of these two steps and try to do perfect Fourth and Fifth Steps. They ruminate, think over and mull upon their wrongdoings. They get wrapped up in the process and do not achieve the results of these steps.

These steps should be taken honestly and quickly. Follow the Fourth Step guide presented below. After an examination of your conscience is made, ask for forgiveness from your Higher Power. Next, call a clergyperson and make an appointment to disclose your wrongdoings.

Fourth Step Guide

There are three aspects of a Fourth Step inventory. They are:

    1) Major shortcomings and wrongdoings.
    2) The Ten Commandments.
    3) Personality defects.

1) Most recovering alcoholics have one or two shortcomings or wrongdoings that bother them intensely. These wrongdoings and shortcomings can get in the way of recovery. So, make a list of major shortcomings and major wrongdoings in your life. Wrongdoings are actions you committed which you know are wrong, shortcomings are actions you should have performed but didn't.

    a) Make a list of major shortcomings. Write out the shortcomings which bother you the most about yourself.

    b) Make a list of major wrongdoings; those wrongdoings you committed that you detest the most.

2) Next look at the Ten Commandments. Read each one. After you read each one carefully, examine your conscience. How does this commandment pertain to your life? Have you violated the commandment? If so, write down the specifics: what, who, when, where and why. Identify your shortcomings and wrongdoings.

    I am the Lord, your God, you shall not have other gods before me.

    You shall not take the name of the Lord, your God, in vain.

    Remember to keep the Sabbath Day holy.

    Honor your father and your mother.

    You shall not kill.

    You shall not commit adultery.

You shall not steal.

You shall not give false witness against your neighbor.

You shall not desire your neighbor's wife.

You shall not desire your neighbor's goods.

3) Make sure your review covers the character defects:

1. Lying—both to others and to self
    a) what kinds of lies
    b) what purpose for the lies
    c) what gain from the lies
2. Stealing—both things and time
    a) what stolen
    b) from whom
3. Sexual area
    a) ignoring spouse
    b) cheating on spouse
    c) promiscuity
4. Laziness—of actions and thoughts
    a) how
    b) when
    c) where
    d) why
5. Hostility
    a) physical
    b) verbal
    c) how
    d) when
    e) where
    f) why
6. Pride—self glory
    a) boasting
    b) showing off
    c) hot-dogging
7. Envy—jealousy
    a) who
    b) what
    c) why

8. Impatience—intolerance
   a) self-centered
   b) self-importance
   c) easily frustrated
9. Self-pity—feelings easily hurt
   a) over-concern for self
   b) selfish
   c) overly sensitive
10. Resentment
    a) who
    b) what
    c) where
    d) why

Having taken a fearless moral inventory, reread your list of wrongdoings and shortcomings. Having reread the list, feel sorrow for having committed thoughts and actions that brought harm to yourself and to others. Next, ask God's forgiveness. Ask to be forgiven of all your wrongdoings and all your shortcomings.

Sometimes recovering alcoholics can identify all their wrongs. They find this causes minimal difficulty. The problem for them is asking forgiveness. Thoughts such as "perfect acts of contrition," or "firm resolve never to commit such acts again," run through their minds. Don't let such perfectionistic thinking get in your way. Make your personal act of contrition with as pure a heart as you can, and *let it be done.*

There are many pamphlets designed to aid one in taking a Fourth Step inventory. They can be beneficial. They can also be a hindrance to healthy, sober living. The purpose of the Fourth and Fifth steps is to unload our past, *not* to pick ourselves apart. Some Fourth Step inventories, however, do more harm than good because they dredge up the past and focus only on failures.

You know who you are and what you did or didn't do. Make a list of your faults and shortcomings and unload them on God and another human being. Make your act of sorrow and then, as soon as possible, see a clergyperson and tell that person your wrongs.

Emotional Growth (Lunch)

Taking a Fourth Step inventory and then a Fifth Step ordinarily creates an intense emotional effect. Feelings can range from embarrassment to relief, from fear to gratitude. Take time now to review your emotional reaction to the Fourth and Fifth Steps of A.A.

How did you feel reviewing your wrongdoings and character defects? Be specific. Were some areas more sensitive than others? Write out your answers.

How can you use these emotions to grow and improve the quality of your life?

Sober Life-Style (Coffee Break)

After you have completed your personal review of your shortcomings and faults, you have "made a searching and fearless moral inventory of yourself." You have taken Step Four of Alcoholics Anonymous.

Do not wallow in self-disgust or pity over your faults and shortcomings. Unload on God and another human being the exact nature of your wrongs. Do this as soon as possible.

We recommend you "take your Fifth Step" with a clergyperson. The reason we encourage you to see a clergyperson is that we are sure whatever you tell the minister, priest or rabbi, will stop there. Nobody else will ever know.

Take your Fifth Step as soon as possible.

Action for the Day (Dinner)

I   Take your Fifth Step today if at all possible. If not, make arrangements with a clergyperson to take your Fifth Step as soon as it is convenient.

II Go to an A.A. meeting.

III At the A.A. meeting, be helpful—help clean up after the meeting, take someone home, make the coffee. Give of yourself at the A.A. meeting.

IV If possible, before or after the A.A. meeting, share with someone you trust and respect that you have taken your Fourth and Fifth Steps.

Feelings: Review of the Day

Sober living is facilitated when we have dealt with those words or actions that were harmful to ourselves or others. Such harmful words or actions were caused by our drinking, were used to defend our drinking, went along with our drinking or even caused our drinking.

Don't feel alone. Everyone, at some time in his or her life does or says something which is harmful to himself or herself or to others. The alcoholic is frequently more aware of the pain of this harm to self or others.

Take this opportunity to relieve yourself of the guilt, shame or whatever negative feelings you may be experiencing. The purpose of the Fourth and Fifth Steps is to review your shortcomings and failures. In other words, to discover your humanness and then to ask for forgiveness from God and from yourself.

Asking forgiveness from God, especially through a minister, is often easier than asking ourselves for forgiveness. This is the essence of the Fourth Step and Fifth Step of A.A., the ability to recognize our failures, to set goals, to live better lives, but most importantly to forgive ourselves—to eliminate guilt and remorse over past actions. If God and others can forgive us, then we can forgive ourselves.

Do you forgive yourself for your wrongs and shortcomings? How do you forgive yourself? Write your answers.

What will you do if guilt and remorse return? How will you deal with feelings, actions and words for which you have already forgiven yourself?

There is no such thing as a perfect Fourth and Fifth Step. Taking the Fourth and Fifth Steps is a start towards a healthy way of life. Many recovering alcoholics review their progress weekly. They praise themselves for all of their successes and thank others who may have helped them. (Have you thanked anyone today for helping you with sober living?) They ask God's forgiveness, for all of their shortcomings and wrong-doings, forgive themselves, and make plans to live better. Step Ten of A.A. helps to establish review of self as a life-style. We will talk more of this later.

If someday you remember something that you forgot to mention in your original Fifth Step, do not panic. Remember, your intentions were to ask forgiveness for all your wrong-doings. So your intentions were honest. What you now remember was included by intention. However, if the newly remembered incident bothers you, take another Fifth Step.

How do you feel about the Fifth Step? What immediate value did it have for you? What future value will it have? Be specific. Write your answer.

Do you feel the practice of a weekly life review would be good for you? If so, why? If not, why not? Read Step Ten of A.A.—"Continued to take personal inventory and when we were wrong promptly admitted it."

One final word about forgiveness. You have taken the time and paid the price to ask for God's forgiveness and to forgive yourself, now don't be ashamed or timid to say you're sorry to those you've hurt or to make amends when you can. Of course, prudence and discretion should determine when you need to apologize, and when it is best to leave things alone. When you can say you're sorry, do so. Also, as you forgive yourself, be charitable enough in your thoughts and actions to forgive others who may have hurt you.

Are you holding grudges? What can you do to get rid of your grudges? Make a plan of action to eliminate grudges, grievances or resentments. Write it out.

What will you do if a grudge, grievance or resentment pops up in your life? How will you deal with it? How will you get rid of it?

Practice feeling good, clean and relaxed. You have accomplished a lot today. Tonight while lying in bed, practice your relaxation exercises.

Daily Reading (While getting ready for bed)

Cliches and Drunkalogues

Sometime, when you go to an Alcoholics Anonymous meeting, you will feel that there is no substance to the program. You may feel that the whole experience is shallow, empty and self-serving. You may look around and feel that these are a lot of silly people telling the same old worn-out stories over and over. Sometime you'll reach out to someone and get only a pious platitude or trite cliche.

When you reached out for sober living, nobody promised you a rose garden. You decided yourself to seek a life of independence from alcohol. Just because you're sober, the world hasn't changed. There are still a lot of people who will annoy you greatly. There are still many things that will irritate you. But remember, you chose sober living because you were unhappy with the way you were living. You did not choose sober living in the hope that the world would change.

Some people who benefit from A.A. may get on your nerves. They will repeat expressions like, "Easy does it" or "One day at a time" over and over again. They will repeat these slogans over and over as if to ward off the evil spirit of drinking. These are silly superstitious people who probably have little sense. Ignore them. They will listen to you but they won't hear you. They are too busy being shallow. Avoid A.A. members who thrive on mumbo-jumbo.

There is a place for the A.A. slogans. They can help an individual to keep life in perspective. If the slogans are valuable to you, use them. If they bother you, ignore them. Use what helps you stay sober. Some of the slogans are placed at the top of each day's entry in this workbook. There is a two-fold purpose for this. The first purpose is to introduce you to them. The second purpose is to help you discover if certain slogans help you with sober living.

There is another problem area for some in A.A., it is the drunkalogue. A drunkalogue is the repetition of a drinking history. Many people in A.A. think this is valuable. People who stick to drunkalogues do so because drunkalogues are safe. They are past tense. Everybody can look at the narrator's past and proudly say, "Look how far that person has come." The use of drunkalogues avoids the present. It does not allow an individual to examine his or her sobriety in terms of current growth. Frequently, the drunkalogue communicates this message: "Don't judge me too harshly, look how far I've come." It's an excuse to avoid relating and reaching out in the present.

The drunkalogue is a story of the past. The A.A. meeting is now. Use the A.A. meeting to keep yourself motivated. Express your successes and failures on a day-by-day basis. There is minimal value in comparing today with a year ago. There is more value in comparing today with yesterday. Where am I now? What is good about it? What needs improvement? Make your A.A. time meaningful. Use it to progress through life, not to remember the past.

Reading Review

In two or three sentences, describe the point of today's reading.

How does today's reading pertain to you? Give at least two examples.

Can you implement in your life something from today's reading? Write down how you can implement today's reading in your life.

Evening Reflection (When in bed)

Practice an act of faith in your Higher Power. Today has been emotionally intense for you. You have examined your life and identified your wrongdoings and shortcomings. You have asked God to forgive you and admitted (or made plans to admit) the exact nature of your wrongs to another person. You have also forgiven yourself. Today has been an important day in your recovery from alcoholism.

Practice an act of faith. Let your spirit reach out to your Higher Power and believe in a natural order of things. Believe that there is meaning to your life and your relationship with God as you understand Him.

Contemplate the following act of faith: "Thy will be done…"

Day Thirteen—*Thirty Meetings In Thirty Days . . .*

Morning Meditation (Upon Rising)

Yesterday in the morning meditation, you contemplated faith. Take a moment to renew your faith.

Today we will contemplate hope. Hope assumes that we believe, and helps us set goals and objectives. Hope gives purpose to life. We hope for sobriety, for a sense of well-being and for love. Hope becomes the motivation behind our faith. Hope encourages us to put our beliefs into practice on a daily basis.

This morning look out the window and let your mind think about your hopes. Identify two or three of your essential hopes and formulate them into an act of hope founded on your faith in God and in yourself. Hope reflects your attitudes. Let your hopes be a positive part of your Faith.

Contemplate your hopes.

Make an act of faith in your God and in yourself.

Thinking About Yourself (Breakfast)

Your life probably looks better and you probably feel better about yourself today than you have in the past.

Write a true story entitled, *How It Looks Thirteen Days Later*. In this story, focus on your feelings, thoughts and actions. Describe what they were before you started the program, what has happened to them since you started and the price you've paid for the change. Write in your notebook.

What do you like most about the changes in your life? Write your answers.

What do you feel uncomfortable about in the changes you identified?

What else would you like to change about yourself? Be specific.

Make a plan to implement these changes.

Emotional Growth (Lunch)

Sometimes a recovering alcoholic who realizes the spiritual aspect of recovery has a spiritual crisis. This crisis can come in a variety of forms. Some have great intellectual difficulty believing in God. Others dislike the idea of religious rituals and protocol. Whatever the spiritual crisis, each recovering alcoholic needs to deal with his doubts and develop a sense of spiritual direction.

Usually a spiritual crisis originates in our feelings and manifests itself in our thoughts and actions. We think, we intellectually believe, and come to grips with ourselves, our life, our world and our universe. We then become comfortable and complacent in our beliefs. There is then a need to challenge this intellectual complacency. Is it actually pride? Is it a lack of humility?

John Milton in his epic poem *Paradise Lost*, gives the reader his idea of the fall of Lucifer. It is a poignant narrative of Lucifer's arrogance, pride and fear of God. Lucifer, God's greatest creation, when confronted with the opportunity to submit and adore God his creator, refuses to do so and addresses the universe as if he were equal to God. God, in Milton's poem, casts Lucifer out of Heaven. As Lucifer is tumbling into the abyss, he yells out "I'd rather reign in Hell than serve in Heaven."

How sad. Is this your story? Are you holding out for the loneliness of your own hell? Are the intellectual reasons for your spiritual crisis really emotions of fear, pride and arrogance? Are you lacking in humility? Are you attempting to make yourself the center of the universe rather than believing that a Higher Power is the center of the universe? Have you become your own God?

Take time to evaluate your beliefs. What are your spiritual beliefs? Write your answer.

How do you personally relate to these beliefs?

How do these beliefs affect your behavior?

How do you feel about these beliefs?

How can you strengthen and improve the quality of your spiritual beliefs? Are you doing this? If so, how? If not, why not?

How do you express your spiritual beliefs?

How can you improve the quality of your expression of

these spiritual beliefs?

Reread Steps Two and Three of A.A.

Sober Life-Style (Coffee Break)

It may be difficult for you to look at your life objectively now that you have been practicing sober living for fourteen days. You may be experiencing a high feeling because your life looks a lot better. On the other hand, you may feel guilty and depressed because of your failure and mistakes due to drinking. The main thing to keep in mind is that you have been sober for at least fourteen days. You will feel better on some days than on others. Your emotions will vary due to experiences beyond your control. Your sobriety does not have to vary. Sober living is yours as long as you want it. It may not be always wonderful, but in general, because of sober living, your life will be better than it was when you were drinking.

List three aspects of sober living you like most.

List three qualities of sober living you dislike most.

On those days when things go wrong, when that which you dislike about sober living consumes your attention, why and how do you stay sober? Be specific.

If you reread your answers you will probably understand many of your personal beliefs, your reasons for sober living. In three or four sentences, write down your personal beliefs; your reasons for living sober. Let this be your Sober Living Credo.

Action for the Day (Dinner)

I   Go to an A.A. meeting.

II   Take someone out to dinner. If you can't afford that, ask someone to join you for a walk.

III   Get outside and enjoy the day. People who eventually return to drinking frequently slide back to their old ways. This happens because they do not keep active. Healthy thoughts and healthy feelings are reflections of actions. If you are doing activities that are organized, goal-oriented, meaningful and productive, your thoughts and feelings will follow.

The most important thing in the sober living process is to do that which keeps you sober. Do not just think about them. Day in and day out, actually do what keeps you sober.

IV Read your Sober Living Credo.

Feelings: Review of the Day (Beverage Break)

All too often the drinking individual becomes accustomed to feeling badly. This is not limited to physical feelings, it is also a psychological habituation to feeling badly. Feeling badly can become a habit like any other habit.

Learning to feel well, for the recovering alcoholic, requires attention and work. Like any state or habit we want to acquire, we learn to feel well by practice. We break the habit of feeling badly by initiating and developing the habit of feeling well. Feeling badly and feeling well are antagonistic. That is, we usually cannot feel badly and feel well at the same time.

Do those things consistent with your values that make you feel well. When you feel well, recognize it, say "I feel well." If feeling badly slips back, do something consistent with your values to help you feel well. If you are busy and can't do something to arouse good feelings then mentally and emotionally recall good feelings that you have previously felt. Push out the bad feeling by concentrating on a previous good feeling. Feel well.

I   Practice feeling well. Do and think things today that will make you feel well.

II At the end of the day, make a list of things that you did and thoughts that you had that made you feel well. Write it down now.

Do you like feeling well? Do you like to feel good about yourself and your life? Write out your answers.

Describe the experience of feeling well.

What can you do or think to feel a little better? Make specific recommendations.

What have you learned from this day? Give specific observations.

Practice your relaxation training before falling asleep tonight.

Daily Reading (While getting ready for bed)

A.A. - Your Way

Participation in A.A. and the practice of the Twelve Steps of A.A. means sober living for you. You may have been a free-thinking, independent person for most of your life, and your first few contacts with A.A. may have frightened you because of the structure and spiritual values of A.A. You have been told that the A.A. beliefs and participation in A.A. mean sobriety for you. You want to believe this. Does this mean that you have to give up all other beliefs, live only for A.A. and pray and play only with the A.A. crowd?

Concerns about independence and freedom are stumbling blocks for many people who try the A.A. program. The easiest way for some is to plunge totally into an active A.A. life. However, if you can't, if something holds you back, turns you off or drives you away from A.A., this does not mean you have to totally reject A.A.

First, identify for yourself those parts of A.A. (people, actions, attitudes, policies) which you *do* like. Make a list of what you like about A.A. After each item write down how it is beneficial to your sobriety.

Next write down those parts of A.A. that you *don't* like. Is there anything you can do to change the way you feel about those aspects of A.A. which you don't like? Is pride getting in your way? Do you need to practice humility? You have already agreed that many recovering alcoholics benefit from A.A. You also are willing to do whatever will keep you sober. If you are not being prideful and if you truly have problems with some aspects of A.A., perhaps you can compromise and do A.A. your way.

A.A. your way is not a sacrilege. A.A. is for everyone who needs it, but there may be aspects of A.A. that are not for everyone. The chore is to find out what helps you and what causes you problems. The best way to do this may be to find someone in A.A. whom you respect, and discuss with that person your concerns about A.A. Listen carefully and be willing to try what is suggested to you.

There is no rule which says you cannot personalize A.A. You can choose the parts of A.A. that enhance your sobriety. The important thing is to get involved in A.A. Think more about that which assists you than about that which upsets you.

Some people have no difficulty with A.A. until someone tells them they are doing it wrong, or they don't understand or they should do something differently. If you are new to A.A. and find that some parts of A.A. bother you, try to work it out with yourself. One way to cause problems for yourself is to provoke discussions about differences of opinion.

Face it. We all have differences. It is easier for people to find their differences than to find their agreements. Do your soul searching quietly. Do not upset or provoke others who have things worked out for themselves.

Focus on those aspects of A.A. with which you agree and profit from them. Concentrate on what helps you to keep sober. Maximize the assets of A.A. Minimize the liabilities of A.A. Then A.A. will have a chance to aid your sober living. This is doing A.A. your way.

Reading Review

In two or three sentences, describe the point of today's reading.

How does today's reading pertain to you? Give at least two examples.

Can you implement in your life something from today's reading? Write down how you can implement today's reading in your life.

Evening Reflection (When in bed)

1) "We admitted we were powerless over alcohol—that our lives had become unmanageable."
2) "Came to believe that a Power greater than ourselves could restore us to sanity."
3) "Made a decision to turn our will and our lives over to the care of God *as we understood Him.*"
4) "Made a searching and fearless moral inventory of ourselves."
5) "Admitted to God, to ourselves, and to another human being the exact nature of our wrongs."

Spend tonight's reflection meditating on the meaning and value of these five steps to you and to your life.

Day Fourteen—*Let Go And Let God . . .*

Morning Meditation (Upon Rising)

Today, focus on charity—an act of love. Two days ago we thought about faith and yesterday about hope. Charity is the culmination of faith and hope in an act of love; love of God, love of the world around us and love of self.

All too often, the alcoholic gets caught in feelings of hatred, anger and frustration. Recovery from alcoholism means dealing with each of these emotions constructively and acquiring the virtue of love.

Contemplate your love. Make an act of love for God, for those around you and for yourself. Express that love in your morning meditation.

Thinking About Yourself (Breakfast)

You have another day of sober living. You can feel proud of yourself. You are slowly and surely building a history of sober living.

Let's review what you've accomplished so far. Check the following (if completed) and give yourself a grade.

Grades: A   Have accomplished this to the best of my ability.
          B   Have accomplished this well.
          C   Have accomplished this.
          D   Have barely accomplished this.
          F   Have failed to accomplish this.

Check if completed:		Grade	Reaction
_____ a)	Taken Step One of A.A.– "We admitted we were powerless over alcohol, that our lives had become unmanageable."	_____	_____
_____ b)	Called a person who would be happy to find out we were in a self-treatment program and shared this fact with them.	_____	_____

Check if completed:	Grade	Reaction

_____ c)   Made a list of problems we caused for ourselves by our drinking.

_____ d)   Developed a written plan to solve each of these problems.

_____ e)   Identified in writing how our lives are unmanageable due to alcohol.

_____ f)   Identified in writing how we are powerless over alcohol.

_____ g)   Shared with a best friend that we are powerless over alcohol and that our lives were unmanageable due to alcohol.

_____ h)   Spoken at an A.A. meeting.

_____ i)   Reviewed in writing how we used denial to allow ourselves to be alcoholic.

_____ j)   Made a list in writing of our three or four most common techniques for denying our drinking problems.

_____ k)   Taken Step Two of A.A.– "Came to believe that a Power greater than ourselves could restore us to sanity."

Check if completed: <u>Grade</u>   <u>Reaction</u>

_____ l) Taken Step Three of
A.A.–"Made a decision
to turn our will and our
lives over to the care of
God *as we understood
Him."*

_____ m) Practiced telling the blunt
truth every day.

_____ n) Made a plan in writing to
ensure telling the truth.

_____ o) Have been telling the
truth since that plan.

_____ p) Made somebody happy.

_____ q) Written out a sober living
plan.

_____ r) Made sure that our sober
living plan is realistic and
well-balanced and will aid
us to live soberly.

_____ s) Found an A.A. sponsor.

_____ t) Became aware of the
weaknesses of our sober
living plan and jotted
them down.

_____ u) Shared our sober living
plan with another person.

Check if completed: <u>Grade</u>   <u>Reaction</u>

_____ v) Taken Step Four of A.A.-   _____
          "Made a searching and   _____
          fearless moral inventory   _____
          of ourselves."   ____   _____

_____ w) Taken Step Five of A.A.-   _____
          "Admitted to God, to   _____
          ourselves, and to another   _____
          human being the exact   _____
          nature of our wrongs."   _____
                                  ____   _____

_____ x) Met all the goals we set at   _____
          the end of Week I for   _____
          accomplishment during   _____
          Week II.   ____   _____

_____ y) Felt good about our-   _____
          selves.   _____
                                  ____   _____

_____ z) Practiced the art of re-   _____
          laxation.   _____
                                  ____   _____

Emotional Growth (Lunch)

You have spent a good deal of time this week working on the negative aspects of your life. Today's review identifies many positive qualities about you and your life. You have accomplished a great deal. You should have a sense of pride in your accomplishments.

Pride is the emotion we feel when we have accomplished goals or attained objectives we set out to achieve. It recognizes our efforts and motivations. It also recognizes all the help and assistance we have received from others and from God. False pride allows us to deceive ourselves and pretend we did it all by ourselves.

Do you feel a sense of pride in your accomplishments over the past two weeks? If so, describe it. If not, what do you feel, and why do you think you don't have a sense of pride?

Have you acknowledged God and the people who have assisted you in these accomplishments? Who are they? Make a list.

Have you expressed gratitude to God and to others who have assisted you in these accomplishments? If so, how did you do this? If not, why not? When will you express gratitude? Write your answers.

Describe the feeling of healthy pride. How does it differ from false pride?

Sober Life-Style (Coffee Break)

It is good to review your progress periodically. How do you think you are doing with your decision to live soberly? Put your response in your notebook.

What do you need to work on to improve your commitment and success with sober living?

What are the problems you are having with sober living, and what can you do about them?

What did you learn about yourself from the lengthy review you completed earlier today?

How can you apply some kind of weekly review practice to your life?

Do you think you will develop the habit of reviewing your sober living periodically? If so, why? If not, why not?

Action for the Day (Dinner)

I   Find someone you trust and share with them how you are doing at developing a life of sober living. Identify both your successes and your failures.

II At an A.A. meeting, comment on your progress with sober living.

III Do something kind for another person. Try to do it unobtrusively.

Feelings: Review of the Day (Beverage Break)

I   How do you feel after a review of your progress?

II Practice feeling well today. Share your good feelings with another person.

III Tonight, practice your relaxation training before falling asleep.

Daily Reading (While getting ready for bed)

A.A. – "The Right Way"

There are Twelve Steps and Twelve Traditions in A.A. They are carefully worded, but they are open to interpretation. They are guidelines for success in the A.A. program. A.A. is a living, breathing group made up of real people with differences and individuality. The beauty of A.A. is that it works for anyone willing to follow the A.A. program.

At A.A. meetings, you will often find people who know "the right way" for everything in A.A. These people tend to take pigeons (new members), under their wing to teach them "the right way." Whatever their motives, these people frequently do as much harm as good. They tend to frighten newcomers with the rules. They tend to overwhelm pigeons with the traditions of A.A. and with A.A. ritual. They drive many new members away from A.A.

One A.A. group had an individual who was particularly outspoken and self-righteous. The other members dubbed him "Mr. A.A." This was their way of limiting the impact of his rigid and authoritarian style. "Mr. A.A.," however, felt it was approval, and used this verbal support to step up his authority and impact on the group. He totally missed the sarcasm of the title. Eventually, the group began to disintegrate as members went to other groups. "Mr. A.A." himself eventually changed groups because he felt he needed a bigger group.

People like this are detrimental to A.A. They do not understand that A.A. is a very personal and spiritual program. They do not know that the heart and soul of A.A. is the fellowship and love that members give to each other in the form of personal attention and support. You should seek out people in A.A. who manifest a quiet supportive enthusiasm for sobriety. Avoid people who emphasize the rules. These people will harm both you and A.A. by replacing fellowship with a rigid pursuit of "the right way."

A.A. can be invaluable to your sober living. The Twelve Steps of A.A. offer a fundamentally sound and healthy approach to life, and have proven to be a successful tool for sober living with thousands of people. Each person has to discover the degree of participation in A.A. which will be best for his or her life. It is hard to do this alone. When you are new at something, especially something as hard as sober living, you need all the help you can get. However, not everybody who wants to help has the ability to help. It is easy to know who is helpful and who will get in the way of your sober living. It requires nothing more than finding A.A. people who are working the program and people around whom you feel comfortable. If someone makes you feel uncomfortable, do not let that person drive you away from A.A. Instead, ignore that person, avoid being around that person and actively seek out those members with whom you are comfortable.

Remember, no one has the "right way." Each person has to decide how to live the Twelve Steps. Do not let one know-it-all harm your A.A. activities. Think for yourself. Live the Twelve Steps of A.A. in a healthy fashion and seek out A.A. members and an A.A. home group with which you are comfortable.

A.A. members and A.A. groups are like other people and other groups. They come in all sizes, shapes and colors. You need to find an A.A. group with which you blend comfortably. Living your A.A. program is like anything else that is good for you. It takes effort. You will get out of your A.A. program what you put into it.

Reading Review

In two or three sentences, describe the point of today's reading.

How does today's reading pertain to you? Give at least two examples.

Can you implement in your life something from today's reading? Write down how you can implement today's reading in your life.

Evening Reflection (When in bed)

Spend this time tonight thinking about gratitude. You have accomplished much recently. You have come a long way. Feel gratitude in your heart. Mentally picture everyone to whom you are grateful.

Spend a few moments in a prayer of gratitude for your growth and achievement. Express gratitude to God, feel gratitude to all fellow human beings who have helped you.

Think of ways you can show your gratitude. Plan to do so.

Prologue to Week Three

What is sober living? Many recovering alcoholics are concerned that life won't be the same, that life won't be exciting. Some are even afraid they won't like sober life.

These are common concerns for individuals recovering from alcoholism. There is no uniform solution for these concerns. Sober living is a combination of who you are and what you make of sober living. Sober living is what you make it.

There is an old adage around Alcoholics Anonymous, which reads something like this: "If you sober up a drunken horse thief, you have a sober horse thief." Quitting drinking won't change who you are. If there are aspects of yourself that are harmful to you or others, the only way to change them is to change your habits.

Sober living is what you make it. Putting a plug in the jug and practicing the Twelve Steps of A.A. won't solve all your problems. Granted, putting the plug in the jug and practicing your A.A. program are the essential first steps. But if you want more out of life than the same old life-style without booze, you have to do something. You have to change. You have to do the things that will make you feel the way you want to feel. You have to do the things that let you be the person you want to be.

We are not talking about changing your personality. We are talking about habits which hinder or impair happy living. For example, do you harbor resentments toward others? If so, do these resentments make you happy, angry or irritated?

The only way to solve the problem and to feel better is to get rid of the resentment. You need to develop the habit of avoiding resentments.

During this week, we will talk about problem solving; how to develop a life-style of solving your problems as they occur, rather than allowing them to dominate and harm your sober living.

What is sobriety for you? Anything you want it to be. If you want more out of life than just sobriety, you must do something to achieve it. If you want your life to be happy and sober, you must develop the ability to live happily.

Today you begin your third week of practicing sober living. So far you should have accomplished the following actions:

I   Taken the First Step of A.A.
II   Completed Steps Two and Three of A.A.
III Developed and implemented an honesty plan.
IV   Developed a sober living plan.
V   Found an A.A. sponsor.
VI   Taken the Fourth and Fifth Steps of A.A.

If you have not completed one of these six actions—DO IT!—NOW!!

If you have completed these six actions you deserve congratulations, you are progressing nicely.

Take a moment to review the purpose of each section of the workbook.

Morning Meditation—A brief moment alone preparing yourself for the day.

Thinking About Yourself—Intellectual reflection on your drinking, your life and your sobriety.

Emotional Growth—Identifying feelings which need development.

Sober Life-Style—Planning and learning skills which will maximize sober living.

Action for the Day—Putting into practice activities that keep you sober.

Feelings: Review of the Day—Developing the habit of monitoring your emotional reaction to each day.

Daily Reading—Gathering information about alcoholism and recovery.

Evening Reflection—The practice of reviewing your progress in sober living each day.

Keep in mind that sober living is well-balanced living. There will be many times when you have an impulse to do two sections at once, or to find excuses to skip a section. Practice self-discipline. Do each section as it is scheduled to be done. Establish the rhythm of sober living by doing every day all that has to be done. If you are not in a treatment program, stick to your own schedule.

Your A.A. Program so far:

1) "We admitted we were powerless over alcohol—that our lives had become unmanageable."

2) "Came to believe that a Power greater than ourselves could restore us to sanity."

3) "Made a decision to turn our will and our lives over to the care of God, *as we understood Him.*"

4) "Made a searching and fearless moral inventory of ourselves."

5) "Admitted to God, to ourselves, and to another human being the exact nature of our wrongs."

Day Fifteen—*Live and Let Live . . .*

Morning Meditation (Upon Rising)

Many people go through life bouncing from one problem to another. They seem never to get on top of their world. They seem always to be reacting to one problem after another.

In general, it is fair to say that there are two kinds of people—problem creators and problem solvers. Problem creators are people who sit back and react to problems or wait for them to go away. Some problem creators react to problems in a way that creates more problems.

A problem solver, however, is any person who quickly notices a problem, identifies the exact nature of the problem, and sets goals to solve the problem. A problem solver develops a plan that will solve the problem. Then, he or she implements the plan and reviews to see that the problem was satisfactorily solved.

Steps to being a problem solver

1) Identify the exact nature of the problem.
2) Set goals as to how you want to solve the problem.
3) Develop a plan of action that will allow you to reach that goal.
4) Implement the plan of action.
5) Review to see that the problem has been solved the way you want it solved.

Thinking About Yourself (Breakfast)

In general, problem areas can be divided into four categories: money, job, marriage and sex, and other personal problems.

Money

For many people, this is the number one problem. You have to be careful with this problem because it is easy to say you have a money problem when the real problem might be something slightly different. For example, do you spend too much money and pile up bills? Do you have a job that doesn't pay enough and never will? Is your money problem really due to your drinking and if you would stop drinking the money problem would slowly resolve itself? In other words, if your problem is money, what is the exact nature of the money problem?"

Job

What is it you don't like about the job? Is it the type of work? Is it the boss? Is it the hours worked? Is it the pay? Is it everything? What options do you have? Can you find a better job? Can you get a raise? A promotion? A change in supervisors? What is the problem and what do you want to do about it?

Marriage and Sex

Many people complain of problems in this area of life. Yet they have difficulty in being specific. Are there difficulties in your marriage or sex life? Keep in mind that although marriage and sex life overlap, they are not identical. Marriage includes much more than sex, such as shared responsibilities, communication in non-sexual ways, and love.

What is it you don't like about your marriage or sex life? What options do you have to solve these problem areas? Do you need professional advice?

Other Personal Problems

There are many different types of personal problems. They come in all sizes and shapes. First, you have to define the precise nature of the problem.

Some suggested questions are given below which you can ask yourself in attempting to define personal problems. Write "yes" if the problem pertains to you.

1. Is self-pity a problem for you?   _____
2. Are you critical of others?   _____
3. Are you insincere?   _____
4. Do you procrastinate?   _____
5. Are you lazy?   _____
6. Do you envy others?   _____
7. Do you gather resentments?   _____
8. Are you a grievance collector?   _____

9. Are you impatient? _____
10. Are you dishonest? _____
11. Do you smile too much? _____
12. Are you too kind? _____
13. Are you filled with self-importance? _____
14. Do you hate? _____
15. Do you make excuses for yourself? _____
16. Do you dwell on vulgar thoughts? _____
17. Do you spend time trying to get even with others? _____
18. Do you let the success of others upset you? _____
19. Are you a goody-two-shoes? _____
20. Are you prompt? _____
21. Are you too humble? _____
22. Are you modest? _____
23. Are you straightforward? _____
24. Are you patient with yourself? _____
25. Are you active enough? _____
26. Do you trust those close to you? _____
27. Do you practice healthy thinking? _____
28. Are you generous with your time and possessions? _____
29. Are you charitable in your thoughts about others? _____
30. Do you forgive others? _____
31. Do you love yourself? _____
32. Do you take care of yourself? _____
33. Do you practice positive thinking? _____
34. Do you practice negative thinking? _____
35. Are you jealous of others? _____
36. Do you put yourself down? _____
37. Are you too easy on yourself? _____
38. Are you too hard on yourself? _____
39. Do you harbor grudges? _____
40. Do you lie? _____

Review those items you checked. Now begin to make sense out of them. You'll find that many of these items are related. Try to define the areas of your life which create a personal problem for you. For example, it might be an attitude problem. Maybe your resentment causes you to isolate yourself and feel bitter. The idea is to find the problem. Then set out to solve the problem. Now that you have given a lot of thought to life problems fill out the Personal Problem Solving Rating Scale.

Personal Problem Solving Chart

The following are problems that people have in their lives. This is an aid to help you formulate problem areas in your life. Please rate each of these items on the scale from 1 to 7. 1 means the item causes you no difficulty at all, 7 means the item is a major life problem for you. *Circle* your rating for each item.

	No Problem					Major Problem	
1. Self-confidence	1	2	3	4	5	6	7
2. Impulsiveness	1	2	3	4	5	6	7
3. Expressing anger	1	2	3	4	5	6	7
4. Getting up on time	1	2	3	4	5	6	7
5. Ability to meet new people	1	2	3	4	5	6	7
6. Keeping appointments	1	2	3	4	5	6	7
7. Financial matters	1	2	3	4	5	6	7
8. Feelings of unworthiness	1	2	3	4	5	6	7
9. Sleeping	1	2	3	4	5	6	7
10. Talking to other people	1	2	3	4	5	6	7
11. Keeping the kids together	1	2	3	4	5	6	7
12. Being cheerful	1	2	3	4	5	6	7
13. Eating	1	2	3	4	5	6	7
14. Listening to other people	1	2	3	4	5	6	7
15. Expressing love	1	2	3	4	5	6	7
16. Doing a good job	1	2	3	4	5	6	7
17. Working with others	1	2	3	4	5	6	7
18. Being understanding	1	2	3	4	5	6	7
19. Being likeable	1	2	3	4	5	6	7
20. Being alone	1	2	3	4	5	6	7
21. Being selfish	1	2	3	4	5	6	7
22. Communicating with others	1	2	3	4	5	6	7
23. Family responsibility	1	2	3	4	5	6	7

		No Problem					Major Problem	
24.	Self-control	1	2	3	4	5	6	7
25.	Obligations	1	2	3	4	5	6	7
26.	Patience	1	2	3	4	5	6	7
27.	Feeling rushed	1	2	3	4	5	6	7
28.	Inability to relax	1	2	3	4	5	6	7
29.	Neighbors	1	2	3	4	5	6	7
30.	Temper	1	2	3	4	5	6	7
31.	Work	1	2	3	4	5	6	7
32.	Leisure time	1	2	3	4	5	6	7
33.	Problems with spouse	1	2	3	4	5	6	7
34.	Getting to work on time	1	2	3	4	5	6	7
35.	Enjoying yourself	1	2	3	4	5	6	7
36.	Finding non-drinking friends	1	2	3	4	5	6	7
37.	Depression	1	2	3	4	5	6	7
38.	Marital problems	1	2	3	4	5	6	7
39.	Gossip	1	2	3	4	5	6	7
40.	Car trouble	1	2	3	4	5	6	7
41.	Friends	1	2	3	4	5	6	7
42.	Boss	1	2	3	4	5	6	7
43.	Loneliness	1	2	3	4	5	6	7
44.	Fear	1	2	3	4	5	6	7
45.	Day-dreaming	1	2	3	4	5	6	7
46.	Lots of plans, but no actions	1	2	3	4	5	6	7
47.	Legal problems	1	2	3	4	5	6	7
48.	Accepting help	1	2	3	4	5	6	7
49.	Trusting others	1	2	3	4	5	6	7
50.	Feelings of guilt	1	2	3	4	5	6	7

Spend some time to review the patterns of your scores on the Personal Problem Solving Checklist. Does there appear to be a pattern. Do your problems tend to be internal, such as feelings? Do your problems tend to be interpersonal, such as problems with a person or persons? Do your problems tend to be external, such as problems with bills?

Frequently, a person will have a style of problem. Identifying the type of problem you have allows you not only to understand yourself better, but also to set sharper and clearer strategies of problem solving. Look at those items you scored 5 or more. Make a list of those items. Try rearranging the list to see the similarity between items.

Emotional Growth (Lunch)

Looking at the problem areas of your life can have a negative emotional impact. It might make you depressed or nervous. Having looked at the problem areas of your life, how do you feel? Write your answers.

Which problem area embarrasses you, or makes you feel the most discomfort? Describe how you feel about this problem area.

How can you profit from your emotional reaction to looking at your problems?

Sober Life-Style (Coffee Break)

Now from the list of those items scored 5 or more that you have rearranged into common areas, make a list of the three largest problem areas you have, other than alcoholism.

Below, begin to solve these three problems. Write out your answers. Write the name of problem #1.

A) Exact nature of problem. Describe it fully.
B) Set goals. (How would you like to solve the problem?) Be specific.
C) Develop a plan to solve the problem. Be as detailed as possible.
D) Put the plan into action as soon as possible. Write down a timetable for problem solving. When will you start? When will you do each step? Be as specific as possible.
E) Review your progress daily.

Write the name of problem #2 and problem #3 and continue the process of solving them as you did for problem #1.

Everybody has problems. Sober living requires that an individual work daily to solve problems as they arise. Some time ago, an older man went through a rehabilitation program.

At the end of treatment, he said that one of the most important things he learned while in treatment was that there is no difference between winners and losers in this world, except one. When asked what that one difference was, he said, "Well, winners and losers both make mistakes, but winners do not repeat their mistakes, losers do." There is truth in this thought. The ability to have a successful life rests on the ability to learn from mistakes.

Become a problem solver. There is nothing to it. Essentially, it requires an attitudinal change. Instead of suffering from your problems, you decide to do something about them.

This is the strategy for problem solving:

1) Identify the problem.
2) Decide how you want to solve it.
3) Develop a plan to achieve that solution.
4) Implement the plan.
5) Review your results.

Action for the Day (Dinner)

I   Attend an A.A. meeting.

II Read about sober living in an appropriate book for 60 minutes.

III Write one paragraph describing what you read and what you got from it.

Feelings: Review of the Day (Beverage Break)

I   How does it feel to be in the third week of sobriety? Write your answer.

II What have you done today (thoughts or actions) to make yourself feel good?

III Was it successful? Why was it successful? Was it unsuccessful? Why was it unsuccessful?

IV What have you done today to make another person feel happy? If you have done nothing, do something now.

During the first week of treatment you focused on feeling good. You practiced bringing this feeling upon yourself.

During the second week you practiced feelings of relaxation. These are two excellent exercises. The first is developing good feelings about yourself and a sense of comfort with yourself. The second is developing the ability to let go and to relax within yourself. This week we will practice feeling a sense of accomplishment.

Place yourself in a quiet place. Think about what you have done over the past two weeks. Practice feeling good about yourself. Let your mind focus on the thought of yourself as a successful person. At the same time practice feeling relaxed. Keep in mind these are two feelings you can bring upon yourself.

Now, as you are feeling good, feeling relaxed, review in your mind the good things you've accomplished over the past two weeks. Feel a sense of accomplishment. You've done it. Praise yourself.

Daily Reading (While getting ready for bed)

Grievance Collectors

Grievance collectors are unhappy people. They go through life looking for slights and wrongs. Essentially, grievance collectors are people who want everyone to bow and scrape in front of them. They want others to think only good and pure thoughts about them. They want people to be always kind and understanding. They want to live in a perfect world, where everyone is good, sweet, just, and where not a disparaging word is heard.

The grievance collector goes through life waiting for someone to slight or harm him. Then the grievance collector harbors resentment and bad feelings for whoever slighted him or hurt or lied to him.

The best way to be unhappy in this life is to depend on others for approval and support for everything. If you want to be unhappy, make a list of people who did not recognize you for all your merits. Put at the top of the list those who gossiped about you or said things to belittle your efforts. If you want to be unhappy, condemn them for not giving you total support for all you do. If you do all these things, you will be unhappy.

What can you do if you are the kind of person who is bothered by the words or actions of another person? What if words don't roll off you like water off a duck's back? What if you are the kind of person who naturally is upset and bothered when you are slighted? What if you tend to seethe when people show you up or get more than is fair?

First of all, recognize that you are not alone. There are many, many people just like you. There are many people who tend to be grievance collectors, who gather resentments and seethe in anger. However, recognizing that you are not alone does not solve the problem. It does give hope. The hope is that if other people are able to deal with their resentments, you too can learn to solve the problem of resentment.

The second step is to recognize that the problem is yours. The way you look at the world and the way you look at yourself causes the problem. Most people who seethe with resentment lack humility and have an exaggerated sense of themselves. They suffer from false pride. Most of us are average people. Accepting that we are average is difficult. We need much more attention, more respect and more status. The lack of this recognition is the core of most resentment.

Only a thorough understanding of ourselves, a realistic picture of who and what we are will give us the strength to be above resentment or grievance. A realistic understanding of ourselves will come only through constantly checking our actions. Many people use repeated Fourth and Fifth Steps as a way of developing a wholesome knowledge of themselves. Some use a spouse who gives feedback and makes comments and observations. Some people use group psychotherapy to learn about themselves. If you are a person who tends to collect grievances and gather resentments, you need to do something about it. This problem will not go away by itself.

There are times when people do or say things that are unjust and harmful. If you are affected, do something about it. Don't sit and seethe, solve the problem. The solution may require some assertiveness on your part, but it will be worth it.

Assertiveness is the ability to stand up for yourself and solve your problems without acting like a bull in a china shop. Some people go overboard with assertiveness, they become abrasive and obnoxious. Other people use assertiveness to cover up hostility and aggression. These are misuses of assertiveness.

If you think you lack the ability to solve the interpersonal problems which are at the root of your resentments and grievances, then perhaps you need assertiveness training. There are opportunities in most communities for assertiveness training workshops. If you plan to attend one, check the credentials of those who offer the workshop. There are also a number of paperback books that are available on assertiveness training. Remember, anyone can write a book, so review the credentials of the author and don't believe everything you read.

Essentially, assertiveness is a way of solving interpersonal problems. The goal is to solve the problem. Like most problem solving, it starts with an identification of the exact nature of the problem. What is the problem? Who is causing it? What are they doing? When are they doing it? Where and how are they doing it?

The second step is to set goals. How do you want this problem solved? What are your options? Do you want the person doing something to stop it? Do you want a rumor corrected? Do you want attention or recognition for something? What do you want?

The third step is to develop a plan to solve the problem. Do you have to do something? Do you need to say something to someone? What steps need to be taken to solve the problem? Solving most grievances and resentments will require you to confront people about their behavior. Remember, your goal is to solve the problem, not create additional problems. Therefore, your confrontation needs to be done in a way that solves the problem but allows the other person to save face or bow out gracefully. If you are loud, angry, or hostile in your confrontation, you may not only fail to solve the problem, but you may even create additional problems.

After you have developed your plan, implement it. Put your thoughts into action. The solution may not be perfect but it will be better than sitting around and seething about your grievance or resentment. Follow your plan. The action alone will reduce the pain of most resentments.

If you can't solve the resentment or grievance, then the problem is yours. Look at yourself honestly. You probably have an inflated sense of your own worth and importance. This is your problem. Do something to get in touch with yourself. See yourself as others see you. Use others to sharpen your perception of yourself.

Reading Review

In two or three sentences, describe the point of today's reading.

How does today's reading pertain to you? Give at least two examples.

Can you implement in your life something from today's reading? Write down how you can implement today's reading in your life.

Evening Reflection (When in bed)

Contemplate the meaning and value to you of the Third Step of Alcoholics Anonymous.

Step Three—"Made a decision to turn our will and our lives over to the care of God *as we understood Him.*"

Day Sixteen—As We Understood Him . . .

Morning Meditation (Upon Rising)

Last week you took your Fourth and Fifth Steps of A.A. You made a searching and fearless moral inventory, then you admitted to God, to yourself and to another human being the exact nature of your wrongs. Many recovering alcoholics feel tremendous emotional relief after taking good Fourth and Fifth Steps. During this morning's meditation, think about Steps Six and Seven. Think how they relate to your life and to your recovery from alcoholism.

Step Six—"Were entirely ready to have God remove all these defects of character."

Step Seven—"Humbly asked Him to remove our shortcomings."

Thinking About Yourself (Breakfast)

Problem solving as a way of life requires a daily intention to solve problems when they happen. Most people do not live this way. Most people tend to put off solutions until some vague future time. Some people even enjoy the turmoil caused by the problem in their lives.

By now you should have solved the three problems that you identified yesterday. (You did solve those problems DIDN'T YOU?) Or maybe you think that some problems can't be solved immediately. You're wrong. Any problem you identify can be solved immediately, if you want to solve it.

Granted, the solution may require continual effort over a long period of time, but the problem is solved. It is no longer festering. If a problem is being worked on, it is solved for as long as you continue to work on it. As long as you advance, you are winning.

Let's look at an example of a BIG problem that can be solved in one day as long as it is worked on every day for a long time. We will take the problem of bills and, following our problem solving philosophy, we will solve the problem.

I   Identify the exact nature of the problem.
  A. The name of the problem is bills.
  B. The exact nature is I owe so much money I can't manage all of my bills.
  C. I make $900 a month, take home, and to exist I need:

Rent	$300
Utilities	$100
Phone	$ 50
Food	$200
Car Payment and Gas	$150
Sub Total	$800

  I also owe:

Department Store	$50 a month on a balance of $600
Credit Cards	$25 a month on a balance of $225
Other Charge	$35 a month on a balance of $400
Small Bills	$60 a month

Sub Total	$170
Back Bills	$170
Living Expenses	$800
TOTAL	$970

  D. If you think you can't solve the problem because you owe more money than you make, you're wrong. If you want to solve the problem, continue with problem solving philosophy.

II   Having identified the exact nature of the problem, you must now set goals. How do you want to solve the problem? I want to get ahead on my bills and live within my means.

III   Now, having identified the exact nature of the problem (you clear $900 a month and owe $970 a month), and having identified how you want to solve this problem (to get caught up on bills and live within my means), you must next develop a plan to solve this problem.

Plan

1. To pay bills on a regular, monthly basis.
2. To cut down use of the telephone and lights and gas, hoping to save $10 a month.
3. To restrict use of the car until caught up on the bills,

hoping to save $10 a month.

4. To exercise and cut down on eating. (Most Americans eat more than they need.) Also, to stretch food buying a little more hoping to save $10 a month.

5. To take a part-time job on nights or weekends that will bring in $20 a week, which would be $80 a month. To take a job pumping gas, delivering for a store, bagging at a grocery store. Any small part-time job will do, don't let pride get in the way.

6. This plan will save $30 a month from existing bills and will add $80 a month from the part-time job.

7. Income will be increased to $980 a month and expenditures will be reduced to $940 a month.

8. Whatever is left over (in this case $40), we will put in the bank for a rainy day. If there are no rainy days we will *not* touch this money until we are caught up on our bills.

9. We will create no new bills *until* we are caught up.

10. This plan will take twelve months to pay the final department store payment.

IV Having made a plan, the next step is to implement it *NOW*.

A. Go find a part-time job.

B. Cut back on gas and lights, etc.

C. Share your plan with another person.

D. DO IT—*NOW!*

V Having identified the exact nature of the problem; having set a goal; having made a plan to solve the problem; having begun to work the plan, the next thing is to review your success at solving your problem. Preferably this will be done with another person. Review the results of your plan daily until you're well under way and then review it at least weekly until the problem is over.

This is only an example. Your problems may be different or more complex, but this style of problem solving works, if you are willing to practice it daily.

List the three problems you identified yesterday. Write in your notebook. Is your plan for each problem as detailed and specific as the example we have just presented? If it is, give yourself a grade for each problem solving plan of action. Write in your notebook.

Grades:

A   Will definitely solve my problem
B   Probably will solve my problem
C   Might solve my problem
D   Can't really tell if it will
F   Won't solve my problem

If your plan is not as specific and detailed as the example we gave, or if you gave yourself a grade less than an A, do your problem solving over again. It must be specific and you must be confident it will work. Write out your answers.

Exact nature of the problem: Name of Problem #1.

A.   Goals for the problem. (How do you want to solve the problem?)
B.   Develop a specific plan of action to solve the problem.
C.   Put the plan into action—NOW. Write down when you will do it. Be specific.
D.   Review progress daily.

Exact nature of the problem: Name of Problem #2.

A.   Goals for the problem. (How do you want to solve the problem?)
B.   Develop a specific plan of action to solve the problem.
C.   Put the plan into action—NOW. Write down when you will do it. Be specific.
D.   Review progress daily.

Exact nature of the problem: Name of Problem #3.

A.   Goals for the problem. (How do you want to solve the problem?)
B.   Develop a specific plan of action to solve the problem.
C.   Put the plan into action—NOW. Write down when you will do it. Be specific.
D.   Review progress daily.

Emotional Growth (Lunch)

Step Six—"Were entirely ready to have God remove all these defects of character." For many a recovering alcoholic, the initial thought of this step causes some emotional discomfort.

The emotions of pride, denial, and humility are at the core of the Sixth Step. Some people go overboard and want to emphasize all their negative attributes and minimize their positive qualities. Others tend toward the opposite extreme. They become defensive about the existence of any character defects. They want to deny their defects.

Humility is the quality which allows us to see ourselves as we are. It is the ability to feel comfortable with our positive attributes. It is also the ability to identify our character defects, state them simply, and truly desire to overcome them.

Are you ready to have God remove all your defects of character? If so, how does that feel? If not, why not? Write your feelings in your notebook.

Read the Sixth Step of A.A. again. Think about yourself. Identify your strengths. Now focus on your character defects. Let the spirit of God *as you understand Him,* pervade your heart and soul. Ask to be ready to have God remove all your defects of character. Describe how you feel about readying yourself for God to remove all your defects of character.

Having prepared yourself to have God remove your defects of character, the next step comes naturally. Step Seven—"Humbly asked Him to remove our shortcomings." This does not require any elaborate prayer or preparation. The step is straightforward and simple. Humbly ask God to remove all your shortcomings. How do you feel? Write out your feelings.

Close your eyes and ponder. Feel close to God, your spirit and the world around you. Feel the good feelings of sober living.

Sober Life-Style (Coffee Break)

What is the value of the Sixth and Seventh Steps of Alcoholics Anonymous in your life? Write it down.

How can you implement these two steps in your life on a regular basis? Be specific.

Action for the Day (Dinner)

I   Go to an A.A. meeting.

II   Before or after the meeting, seek out an experienced A.A. member and discuss problem solving with this person. Don't expect him or her to go about solving problems in the same manner as suggested here, but try to learn how that person, who is successful at sober living, solves his or her problems.

III Do a favor for someone today. Try to do it in such a way that no one knows. Do it for yourself, not for praise.

Feelings: Review of the Day (Beverage Break)

Isn't sober living hard work at times? Write your answers in your notebook.

Have you had a moment yet when you were bored or tired with sober living?

Have you ever felt like throwing it all away and going drinking? Is so, write down the details of how it felt, how you handled it, why you didn't go drinking and how you will handle this kind of feeling in the future. If you have not had a feeling of chucking it all and going drinking, write down why you think you have not felt this and what you will do if you ever get this feeling. Practice feeling a sense of accomplishment. Find a place to be alone. Review your accomplishments and feel good about them. If there are things that you did not accomplish today, make plans to accomplish them tomorrow.

I feel happy with myself.

I feel relaxed.

I feel I'm living a successful life.

Daily Reading (While getting ready for bed)

Guilt

There isn't an alcoholic alive who does not experience some degree of guilt. These guilt feelings are usually related to things the alcoholic said or did while drinking or drunk, the things he or she wishes could be erased or done over.

What is guilt? It is two things, it is a perception of being in the wrong or of having done something that was either morally or legally wrong. It is an emotional reaction to some incident or situation for which we perceive responsibility and in which we were wrong. There is both healthy guilt and unhealthy guilt. Healthy guilt is the perception that you did something wrong, learning from the experience, making amends to the affected individual and resolving to improve your life and avoid such wrongdoing again. Unhealthy guilt is the emotional reaction to perceived wrongdoings—real and imagined—and obsessive, repetitive feelings of dirtiness, badness or shame. This kind of unhealthy guilt reaction prepares an individual for more problems. The individual gets stuck on a psychological merry-go-round. He feels guilty. He does nothing about it. He feels guilty about doing nothing.

Guilt is an emotional reaction we all have from time to time because we all make mistakes periodically. If we ignore guilt feelings, they may go away, or they may not go away. It is necessary to say at this point that guilt is a serious psychological problem for some alcoholics. If you tend to feel guilty a lot, if guilt feelings keep you from feeling clean and whole, if guilt is a way of life for you, then go do something about this obsession with guilt. Don't let guilt dominate your life, do something about it. You may need professional help. However, a self-help book on overcoming guilt may be all you need.

If guilt is only a periodic problem for you, there are some steps you can take to eliminate the destructive effects of unhealthy guilt in your life. Of course, the first step is to avoid creating any new guilt. You do this by living a life that is as free as possible from purposeful wrongdoing. Having avoided creating any new guilt, the next step is to deal with continuing guilt-feelings from past actions. How do you do this? First realize that guilt and other repetitive thoughts and feelings feed on themselves. If you do something wrong, identify it and make amends for it.

Children who do something wrong and are punished for it rarely experience guilt. They did something wrong, got punished, and it's over. Adults, on the other hand, do something wrong and anticipate getting found out or being punished. This apprehension amplifies their guilt. To short-circuit guilt you must recognize your wrongdoing and make amends for it. This requires exposing yourself, but it also allows for two consequences. It allows you to unburden yourself of the guilt feelings that you carry and it sets up a mature life-style that will help you avoid wrongdoing in the future. If you know that you are going to force yourself to make amends afterwards, you reduce the probability of committing a wrongdoing in the first place. To a large extent, dealing with guilt boils down to avoiding actions that will make you feel guilty in the future and making amends for past actions that make you feel guilty now.

Most recovering alcoholics have done things during their drinking days to cover for their drinking or to allow them to go on drinking. They experience guilt feelings as a result of these actions. Recovery from alcoholism is best maintained through the practice of the Twelve Steps of A.A. The Twelve Steps are an excellent means of dealing with guilt. Start with Step Four—"Made a searching and fearless moral inventory of ourselves." This allows the individual to identify wrong-doings. Step Five of A.A. states—"Admitted to God, to ourselves, and to another human being the exact nature of our wrongs." This allows the individual to unload guilt, in other words, to get a clear conscience. Step Eight takes this process a bit further—"Made a list of all persons we had harmed, and became willing to make amends to them all." This step is followed by Step Nine—"Made direct amends to such people wherever possible, except when to do so would injure them or others." These four steps of A.A. are an excellent, healthy way of dealing with guilt. Finally, Step Ten states—"Continued to take personal inventory and when we were wrong promptly admitted it."

Guilt does not have to be a way of life that makes you feel dirty and uncomfortable. Practicing these steps of A.A. will allow you to deal with guilt in a healthy manner.

Reading Review

In two or three sentences, describe the point of today's reading.

How does today's reading pertain to you? Give at least two examples.

Can you implement in your life something from today's reading? Write down how you can implement today's reading in your life.

Evening Reflection (When in bed)

In quiet thought alone, review your day. Feel the growth of sober living within you as you continue to practice it every day. As you reflect upon yourself and your sober living, say a prayer of quiet gratitude.

Day Seventeen—Thirty Meetings in Thirty Days

Morning Meditation (Upon Rising)

Think about being alive. Too often, the recovering alcoholic gets bogged down in thinking about problems. For a few minutes, lift your eyes toward the sky. If the weather permits, go outside. Let your spirits soar. Feel alive. Feel grateful for life. Relate to the world around you. Get yourself ready to meet another day of sober living. Strive to be in touch with your own spirit and your Higher Power at the same time.

Thinking About Yourself (Breakfast)

Much of what we do in life can be governed by how we feel on the spur of the moment. This is not necessarily good or bad, but for the alcoholic, it can be disastrous. We are talking about impulses. Most alcoholics who return to drinking do so on the spur of the moment. They return to drinking on impulse.

It is important for the alcoholic who is practicing sober living to be able to identify feelings and to deal with them in an effective, healthy, mature fashion. What is a feeling? It is something inside us. It's physical. Sometimes we feel in our stomach, sometimes in other parts of our body. But feelings are physical and we literally feel them.

There are happy and sad feelings, pleasant and unpleasant feelings, unspecified and specific feelings. Impulses are particular types of feelings. They are ordinarily feelings that encourage us to do something. They urge us to action.

For the alcoholic practicing sober living there will be impulses to drink. At times they will occur quite frequently. There is no way to get rid of these impulses. They will occur and they will last for a while, only to go away and then come back unexpectedly. Becoming afraid of impulses to drink only increases the frequency of their occurrence.

The first step when dealing with an impulse to drink is to recognize that you have one. Sometimes the impulse to drink will be straightforward. You will feel like drinking. You will feel that sober living is not worth it or you will be so mad you want to get drunk. In these instances, you will know you have an impulse to drink.

Sometimes the impulse to drink will not be so obvious. You will feel that you are on edge, nervous or "antsy." You might feel like exploding or picking a fight. Sometimes you might just feel good.

When dealing with an impulse the first step is to recognize it. When you are not sure, play it safe and treat your feeling as an impulse to drink. After you recognize that you have an impulse to drink, the second step is to describe to yourself, out loud, what is happening. Say to yourself, "I am having an impulse to drink." This is an important step. It puts the impulse in its place. It tells you what you're dealing with. Also, in a way, it diminishes the impulse. It takes it out of the category of vague feelings and puts it into the category of impulses to drink.

The third step in dealing with an impulse to drink is to share it with another person. Tell someone, like a sponsor, a spouse, an A.A. friend. Tell someone who understands that you are having an impulse to drink. Sharing an impulse cuts its intensity in half. You're no longer alone with the impulse. The fourth step is to do something that will take your mind off the impulse The more physical the action, the better it will distract you from the impulse. Next, remind yourself that you are an alcoholic. You are powerless over alcohol and your life becomes unmanageable due to alcohol. Then go to an A.A. meeting as soon as you can get to one. Make sure to mention at the A.A. meeting that you are having an impulse to drink.

Impulses to Drink and How to Handle Them

1) Recognize the signs of an impulse to drink.
2) Identify for yourself that you are having an impulse. Say, "I'm having an impulse to drink."
3) Tell another person that you are having an impulse to drink.
4) Get busy doing something to distract yourself.
5) Go to an A.A. meeting.

Describe in writing your last impulse to drink. (How, what, when, where and why.)

When are you most likely to have an impulse to drink? Be specific and detailed.

What are you feeling when you have an impulse to drink? Where inside yourself are you feeling it? Describe the feeling.

Are you in a specific place or situation when you have an impulse to drink? Recall previous impulses to drink. What did they have in common?

Write down *all* that you can think of about your impulses to drink. Make some conclusions. Try to figure out all you can about your impulses to drink.

Develop a plan to handle an impulse to drink. In this plan, be specific. Write down each step you will take to handle the impulse. Make sure you know how you are going to identify the impulse. Follow the five steps to deal with drinking impulses. Personalize this plan as much as possible.

Emotional Growth (Lunch)

Many of the decisions of our lives were made impulsively. This may have been due to our alcoholism, or it may be that we are simply impulsive. This is a good time to examine the role of emotions when we are in the process of making decisions. The emotion most experienced during decision-making is anxiety. Usually the anxiety manifests itself as a call to action or as a call to avoid taking action.

During a lifetime of sober living, we will have to make thousands of decisions. It is good to know your emotional style in decision-making.

1) Do you let emotional energy build until you make a quick, sometimes impulsive decision, usually an affirmative decision?

2) Do you avoid decision-making, letting your emotions vascillate from a sense of impending failure to a sense of success, frequently winding up with no decision?

3) Do you feel fear and impending failure and tend to react by making a negative decision?

These are only three common emotional styles that inter-act with decision-making. Which one describes you most closely? Comment in detail on the emotional content of decision-making. If one of these styles describes you accurately, write it down.

Are you satisfied with the quality of decisions during your adult life? If so, describe how your emotions help you to make good decisions. If not, describe how your emotions interfere with good decision-making.

Is there any way you can use your emotions to make better decisions? Describe how you would like to have emotions involved in your decision-making.

Remember, you cannot avoid the emotional component in decision-making. Recognize that there is emotional energy urging you to act one way or another. This energy is caused by a degree of unrest or discomfort in your world. Some-thing is out of place or askew and requires balancing.

Our minds prefer a balanced world. When it is not balanced, emotional energy arises urging us to do something to balance our world. However, we are also thinking beings, and even though there is an urge to balance something in our world, we have to gather facts, weigh their relative value, measure the impact of our decisions and then decide. Our emotions can help or hinder this process. Sober, mature living requires the ability to recognize our emotions and to include them in the decision-making process.

Sober Life-Style (Coffee Break)

Decisions are frequently turning points in our lives. Your decision to seek treatment for your alcoholism will be one of the most significant turning points in your life.

Even when a decision is made, and even if it is a good decision, there is frequently a tendency to doubt yourself. How do you know you have made the right decision if, after you have made the decision, you have doubts? Do you push all doubts out of your mind? Are decisions cast in bronze never to be reevaluated?

These are difficult questions to which there are no simple answers. The phenomenon of decision-making is followed by an emotional reaction of nagging doubt. If you expect this emotional reaction, you can keep it in perspective. If it is unexpected, you may give this emotional reaction attention it does not deserve and perhaps even undo your decision because of it. For example, your decision to stop drinking alcoholic beverages was a good decision. You have probably already had a negative emotional reaction to this decision, and have thought about changing your mind.

How did it feel? How did you deal with that emotional reaction? How did you stick to your original decision? Write your answers in your notebook.

You were successful in dealing with the emotional reaction to your decision to stop drinking. What can you learn from this experience that you can apply to your future decisions? Be as detailed and as specific as you can.

A wise person realizes that most decisions are not cast in bronze. They can be reversed or altered. In significant areas of life, counsel and advice from people we trust will be important. If you ever reevaluate your decision to quit drinking alcoholic beverages, realize that you are having an impulse to drink. Treat the urge to reassess your commitment to sober living as you would treat any other impulse to drink.

1) Recognize that you are having an impulse to drink.
2) Identify for yourself that you are having an impulse to drink, say "I'm having an impulse to drink."
3) Tell another person that you are having an impulse to drink.
4) Get busy doing something to distract yourself.
5) Go to an A.A. meeting.

Action for the Day (Dinner)
I   Go to an A.A. meeting.
II After the meeting, talk to someone about impulses to drink. Find out how that person handles impulses to drink. Write down how this person handles drinking impulses.

Write down what you learned from this person and how you can apply it to your life.

III Help out after the meeting. Clean the ash trays, wipe the tables, maybe clean the floors. Do something that needs to be done. What did you do?

IV Telephone someone you haven't talked to in a while. Find out how that person is doing. Practice listening. Tell that person how well your life has been going. Who did you call? Describe the conversation.

Feelings: Review of the Day (Beverage Break)

Sober living does not mean always feeling good. It is the ability to deal with our feelings in an effective and sober way. Don't be afraid or anxious about negative feelings. Remember, feelings are neither moral nor immoral. What is moral or immoral is the way we deal with our feelings.

Identify some negative feelings you've had since being sober. How did you deal with them? Were you satisfied with your way of dealing with negative emotions? How could you improve upon your method of dealing with negative emotions?

Identify the growth you've had since sober in dealing with negative emotions. Feel good about this growth. Experience a sense of well-being as you see your ability to deal with emotions becoming stronger and more practiced.

Daily Reading (While getting ready for bed)

Giving and Taking

Everybody gives and takes from the pot of life, so how are alcoholics different? They are different because they become inordinant in their giving and taking. For the drinking alcoholic, taking is done while drinking and giving is done while sober. The giving, when sober, results from guilt or a desire to compensate. The alcoholic is not freely giving of himself or herself, but is over-reacting, over-spending, over-giving. The alcoholic takes in a gulping and grasping manner. The alcoholic demands instead of asks.

It is natural for the recovering alcoholic, who feels he has taken so much, to feel guilty and to indulge others. Usually, in a few days or a week or two at best, the guilt feelings have subsided sufficiently so that there is less and less over-giving. There is a return to balance. For the drinking alcoholic, this becomes a teeter-totter way of life. Overdoing on one end of the scale and then overdoing on the other end of the scale.

Sober living requires that we all give more than we take. There are more takers in this world than givers. The pot of life would run dry if those of us who are trying to balance our lives only gave as much as we take.

Most of us don't need to practice taking. We do it naturally. What we do need to practice is giving. There are two kinds of giving. The first is a life-style of giving. For example, at an A.A. meeting if somebody spills coffee and doesn't wipe it up, if you have a life-style of giving, you will quietly, in an unassuming manner, go and clean it up. The other type of giving is more formal and organized. This is the hour per week you volunteer with the boy scouts, or the weekly visit you make to a nursing home. This type of giving is a special act that you do in a systematic and routine fashion for other people. Usually, this is called volunteer or charity work. We all need to practice both types of giving.

There is one caution in giving. Be careful that you're not the type who gives and counts. People who give and expect to be recognized or reimbursed in some way quickly become bitter and disillusioned. Keep in mind that the only reason you give is to make the world a better place to live.

Reading Review

In two or three sentences, describe the point of today's reading.

How does today's reading pertain to you? Give at least two examples.

Can you implement in your life something from today's reading? Write down how you can implement today's reading in your life.

Evening Reflection (When in bed)

Through faith in myself, I can become victorious over all my problems.

This is not to discredit effort and problem solving. Faith in myself is a spiritual quality, a recognition of my basic goodness and a desire to be a sober, good person.

Think about yourself. Feel the courage that faith in yourself brings to every problem you have. Believe in yourself.

Day Eighteen—Anger

Morning Meditation (Upon Rising)

". . . give us this day our daily bread . . . ." Meditate on this phrase from the Lord's Prayer. What do these words mean? Do they refer only to physical sustenance, or is there more to daily bread than food? Spend your morning meditation outside if the weather permits. If not, look out a window. See the world around you. Let your mind wonder at the entire world. In your mind's eye see a quiet forest clearing, busy city streets, a hungry ghetto and a lonely tundra. Now think of the phrase "give us this day our daily bread." Relate the phrase to yourself, both physically and spiritually. Now relate it to the world around you both physically and spiritually. Toward the end of your meditation, try to achieve a sense of perspective on yourself and the world around you.

Thinking About Yourself (Breakfast)

Yesterday we spoke about impulses to drink. Today we want to expand that topic to talk about feelings.

Many alcoholics have difficulties with feelings. Some alcoholics may have problems expressing feelings. Others may have problems sharing feelings. Many just feel awkward, embarrassed or even ashamed about feelings.

Sober living requires a well-balanced life. We need to be able to express our thoughts, actions, and feelings. Is it difficult for you to experience emotion, feelings or sentiment? Or, do you enjoy experiencing feelings such as closeness, warmth or sadness?

Most people tend either to exaggerate or repress their feelings. Some people tend to ignore their feelings, to push them aside or get rid of them. Emotions bother them, embarrass them or frighten them. Even the feelings of other people cause discomfort. These people repress their feelings.

Some people tend to dwell on their feelings. They are inclined to over-emphasize, embellish or even exaggerate their feelings. These people enjoy feelings and emotions, they attend to emotions and focus upon them. These people sensitize their feelings.

Do you tend to sensitize or to repress your feelings? How did you decide whether you tend to sensitize or repress your feelings? Be specific with examples and details of all of the factors you looked at. Write your answers in your notebook.

How do feelings create a problem for you? List three specific examples.

How do feelings enhance your life? List three specific examples.

How are feelings related to your alcoholism? List three specific examples.

Emotional Growth (Lunch)

Recognizing our feelings, even the most fleeting and ephemeral, is an essential part of healthy emotional living. Before we can manage our emotions we must learn to recognize them. How do you do that? Simple. Learn to ask yourself, "How am I feeling?" The answer to that question will be in your gut not in your thoughts. We literally feel our feelings. We have to teach ourselves to become aware of these sensations called feelings. During the day ask yourself several times, "How am I feeling?" Ask yourself this question at different times and in different situations. Become aware of the large number of different feelings. Learn how to feel. Experience them. Practice identifying your emotions.

Here is a list of feelings. Check those that you have experienced in the past week.

Love	_____	Sick	_____	Hate	_____
Closeness	_____	Sexy	_____	Anger	_____
Warmth	_____	Healthy	_____	Poorly	_____
Comfort	_____	Funny	_____	Draggy	_____
Friendship	_____	Relief	_____	Sleepy	_____
Good	_____	Guilt	_____	Distracted	_____
Amiable	_____	Anguish	_____	Tired	_____
Pleasure	_____	Alive	_____	Conflict	_____
Trust	_____	Relaxed	_____	Bad	_____

Hostility	_____	Aggression	_____	Troubled	_____
Greed	_____	Assertive	_____	Hungry	_____
Energetic	_____	Alone	_____	Dependent	_____
Independent	_____	Lust	_____	Longing	_____
Competitive	_____	Uptight	_____	Secretive	_____
Overpowered	_____	Frightened	_____	Anxiety	_____
Nervousness	_____	Passion	_____	Pain	_____
Hot	_____	Cold	_____	Crowded	_____
Like Crying	_____	Embarrassed	_____	Ashamed	_____
Redfaced	_____	Tingly	_____	Stiff	_____
Welling-up	_____	Determined	_____	Fierce	_____
Pride	_____	Loose	_____	Cool	_____
Confused	_____	Flattered	_____	Beautiful	_____
Ugly	_____	Blue	_____	Sad	_____
Happy	_____	Honest	_____	Clean	_____
Irritable	_____	Frustrated	_____	Envy	_____

From the list above, choose five different feelings you like to experience. Write in your notebook.

Choose five feelings from the list above that you are indifferent toward.

Choose five feelings with which you are uncomfortable.

How do you know when your emotions or feelings are appropriate and healthy? How do you know when your feelings are out of control and you are over-reacting? Be specific in your answer. Give examples, if you can.

How do you know if you are denying your feelings? How do you know if you are repressing your feelings?

How do you know when you are sensitizing your emotions? When do you over-emphasize your emotions?

Write a true story entitled, *How Feelings Affect My Life.* In this story include specific examples of how feelings affect your life. Are you satisfied with the way feelings affect your life? Comment on how you can improve the way feelings affect your life.

Sober Life-Style (Coffee Break)

Steps Eight and Nine of Alcoholics Anonymous relate very well to all this emphasis on healthy emotional living.

Step Eight reads—"Made a list of all persons we had harmed, and became willing to make amends to them all."

Frequently, when people think of emotional growth and responsibility, they think only of themselves. Sober living requires more than this selfish attitude. We all hurt others during our lives. Sometimes this is accidental, sometimes it is purposeful. Emotional growth goes beyond the ability to recognize and deal with our emotions. It includes the ability to recognize and deal effectively with the emotions of those around us. We start by making amends to those whom we have harmed. Make a list of people you've harmed and exactly what you did. Write in your notebook.

Frequently, Step Eight creates an emotional reaction. Some recovering alcoholics experience intense discomfort at the recollection of harmful acts they committed. Others sense an initial emotional relief in simply identifying honestly those whom they have harmed and the way in which they harmed them. Whatever your emotional reaction, you have come halfway. You have identified those whom you have harmed and how you harmed them. Next read Step Nine—"Made direct amends to such people wherever possible, except when to do so would injure them or others."

This is an emotionally important step for growth in sober living. It requires complete honesty as well as good judgment. Not only is it difficult to decide how to make amends, but good judgment is required to distinguish where attempts to make amends may cause more harm than good. The practice of personal honesty is the only way to decide when the decision not to make amends is for the good of the other person and not for the convenience of ourselves. For every person you listed in the Eighth Step, write out a plan for making amends. Be specific in this list. When, where, and how do you plan to make amends? Write in your notebook.

Having prepared yourself by taking your Eighth Step, all that remains is to make amends. Plan not to do it at once. Choose a convenient time for yourself and the other person. Plan a sufficient amount of time. The other person may have a need to talk in depth about you and your recovery.

Honesty and humility are your guide to both the Eighth and Ninth Steps. Periodically review your own feelings as you take these two steps. Practice courage. Do the steps as quickly and as quietly as you can. At all times during your Ninth Step, remember the goal is to recognize the feelings of others. Be truly concerned about other people. If at any time you think your attempt to make amends may cause additional hurt or harm, do not proceed.

Actions for the Day (Dinner)

I   Do something to make somebody feel happy.

II How did you feel after you accomplished this act? Write it down.

III What did you do? Be specific.

IV Attend an A.A. meeting. After the meeting engage someone in conversation. During this conversation talk to the person about how being sober has affected their emotions.

V   Do sixty minutes of reading on alcoholism or sober living. Write a paragraph describing what you have read and what you got out of it.

Feelings: Review of the Day (Beverage Break)

I   Practice feeling good.

II What do you do or think when you practice feeling good? Write down what you do.

III Try to share your good feelings with another person.

IV What did you do or say to share the good feeling with another person?

V   Was your sharing successful? If so, why? If not, why was it unsuccessful? Be specific. Give details.

VI Do a feeling review. Do you feel good about yourself? If not, arouse this good feeling. Do you feel relaxed? If not, relax yourself. Do you feel like a successful, accomplished person? If not, do what makes you feel accomplished.

Daily Reading (While getting ready for bed)

Anger

Many recovering alcoholics become angry just to have a drink. That's right, they avoid the whole issue of deciding to begin drinking again and use an excuse to return to drinking. Anger is probably the single most common emotional excuse for a return to drinking. All too frequently you hear, "The boss made me so mad, I went out and had a drink before something worse happened." Or you hear, "I got so mad at my wife that I had a couple drinks to calm down."

In our culture, in the movies especially, becoming angry and drinking alcoholic beverages go hand in hand. Anger does not have to mean it's time to get drunk. If you want to get drunk, then why ruin it by first getting mad? Just go get drunk. If you get mad, why confuse the issue by getting drunk. If you're angry, there is something to be done, there is something to work through or resolve.

We all get angry. Anger is a healthy natural reaction to certain situations. Like most emotions, anger is neither good nor bad in itself. It is your reaction to anger and the consequences of anger that have value. If you explode, yell and scream, have temper tantrums; if you punish others unjustly; if you punish yourself; if you don't find the source of your anger; then you lose. Most people lose when they become angry. They don't take the opportunity to improve their lives. They don't use the emotion of anger as a way to grow and strengthen their sober living.

How do you handle anger? First recognize that you're mad. Some people deny their anger, others over-react when they're angry. You can usually tell that you're mad by the physical reaction. There seems to be a definite physical reaction that accompanies anger. It can include signs such as a quickening of the heartbeat, a quickening of breathing and altered speech patterns.

In general, we become angry when things don't go our way. Anger comes when we expect something to be one way and it turns out another, or when we want one thing and get another, or when we want to hear one thing and hear another. Sometimes we have good reason to be mad and sometimes our reasons are petty.

The next step after we recognize that we are mad is to try to stop everything and say to ourselves, "Why am I so mad?" Anger has a tendency to run its natural course, therefore, it is difficult (but not impossible) to interrupt the anger process with the question, "Why am I becoming angry?" If you can ask yourself the question, "Why am I getting mad?" you have the opportunity to direct your anger. This is the pivotal point. Ask yourself, "Why am I getting mad?" You can then have a choice. You can:

1.   Choose to get mad and blow your top. You may feel that you have a self-righteous reason for yelling and screaming. Well, then let yourself go. There is only one rule: no physical violence. If you can't promise that your yelling and screaming won't turn into physical violence, then this is *not* one of your options. If you can promise no violence and you choose to blow, then let it go.

2.   Choose to get mad and try to solve the problem. This requires an additional step beyond finding out why you're mad. It requires that you tell the person or persons they are making you mad and that you would like to solve the problem. It is a two-fold step. It starts with a) you are making me mad, and b) I would like to solve this situation. Then you need to implement your problem solving skills.

3.   Choose to ignore the issue. This requires either self-deceit or a very good reason and a lot of resolve. There are times to ignore the issue when something is making you mad. In general, this is unwise and you are probably lying to yourself by saying there is no way you can solve the problem.

Whatever you do, first give yourself a choice. If you ask

yourself, "Why am I mad?", then follow that with, "What do I want to do about it?" you have three basic choices. Whatever you choose, make sure you feel good about it. If you're going to feel guilty afterwards, perhaps you should choose something else.

Recovering alcoholics need to deal with anger. That does not mean that you should never become angry. It simply means you need to deal with anger in ways other than getting drunk or feeling guilty.

Reading Review

In two or three sentences, describe the point of today's reading.

How does today's reading pertain to you? Give at least two examples.

Can you implement in your life something from today's reading? Write down how you can implement today's reading in your life.

Evening Reflection (When in bed)

Read Steps Eight and Nine again. Think about the value of making amends. Try to see the entire process of making amends as a good thing. Think about the cleansing value of making amends and the emotional maturity required to recognize the emotional needs of other people. Finally, reflect upon the emotional growth you've experienced over the past two weeks.

Day Nineteen—And the Wisdom To Know The Difference . . .

Morning Meditation (Upon Rising)

The gift of giving is a talent shared by too few people. Many people are so wrapped up in themselves that they have little time for anyone else. Charity is the virtue of reaching beyond yourself. For the recovering alcoholic, charity is not only a virtue, but a style of life that strengthens sober living. Meditate this morning on people in your world who need your charity. Review the quality of your charity. How can you improve this attribute in your life. Resolve to extend yourself and to practice charity. Plan to practice charity in a special way today, and as part of your life-style every day.

Thinking About Yourself (Breakfast)

Today we will continue our emphasis on feelings. The expression of feelings is essential for sober living. In order to clarify your thinking on feelings, respond to the list of items given below. You probably have strong feelings towards many of them. After each item, write down the feelings you have towards that person or thing. In the next column write down how you express this feeling or how you deal with it. Finally, in the last column, decide if this feeling and the expression of it strengthens your sober living or weakens it. If you have more than one feeling about any of the items, jot down all the feelings you have. Write down all the ways you express these feelings. If you repress the feeling and don't express it, write that down. If you sensitize the feeling and over-express it, write that down.

In your notebook set up the columns shown below:

Person or Situation	Feelings	How You Express The Feeling	Does This Feeling And Its Expression Strengthen Or Weaken Your Sober Living?

At the left of the page list the people and situations shown below and fill in the other columns honestly. Describe your feelings about: Spouse, mother, father, job, boss, sobriety, child #1, child #2, yourself, A.A., best friend, friends in general, your marriage.

Emotional Growth (Lunch)

Throughout this workbook, you have been asked to share thoughts about yourself with other people. You have been asked to reach out to others and do something kind for them. Regardless of how you feel at the time, the act of relating to others is essential to your recovery from alcoholism. Alcoholism is a love affair between you and the sedative chemical alcohol. Together you and alcohol achieved isolation, depression and emptiness. Recovery from alcoholism comes through love in its broader and healthier sense. Recovery is a true love of self, a love of life and a love for those in your life. It is not a gushy sentimental love. Recovery from alcoholism is a love of giving and sharing the good as well as the bad. It is a love of truth, a love of ourselves for who and what we are; a love of those around us for who and what they are. Most of all, it is a love of growth and energy for change; a love for improving and developing to full potential both ourselves and the world around us.

Love starts with truth and simple beauty. Describe your love for yourself. In this description, detail what is good about you and also what you need to continue to develop. Write in your notebook.

In general, are you satisfied with your feelings and the ways you express them? Be specific in your answer.

Are there some areas of feelings, or expression of feelings, that you think you should be working on to strengthen your sober living? If so, what are those feelings and what is your plan to develop a healthier way of expressing those feelings? Be specific. Give your plan in detail.

What do you love about the world around you? Be specific. Identify people, places and things you love.

If you agree that the practice of love is giving, what do you give to yourself, to others around you and to your personal world? Be specific. Are you short on giving? You might take this opportunity to describe what you can give to yourself, to others around you, and to your personal world. Develop a plan for giving.

Sober Life-Style (Coffee Break)

In the section entitled *Thinking About Yourself*, you identified feelings that you have toward people and situations in your world. If you were practicing blunt honesty, you probably had both positive and negative feelings toward each one. For some people this creates discomfort. They are surprised that they can feel love for someone and also feel frustration or another less attractive emotion. This confusion is both the paradox of the human condition and the art of sober, well-balanced living.

The world is not a simple place. There are many shades of gray in all aspects of life. We want, however, to simplify our world. A woman recovering from alcoholism once commented, "Why isn't the world black and white, with simple answers for everything with no complexity and no paradoxes? If it were I would have no problems with recovery."

The A.A. phrase "Keep it Simple" does not mean we should eliminate life's complexities. It means we shouldn't confuse issues by bringing in extraneous and irrelevant matters. It is the same with our emotions. We will feel differently toward the same person at different times, and we will sometimes feel conflicting emotions toward the same person. Momentary anger or frustration does not necessarily alter an abiding emotion of love or happiness. The ability to balance these emotions is fundamental to sober living.

Have you ever experienced conflicting emotions toward someone? If you have, how did you handle this emotional condition? Write a description of your feelings. You may want to think of your spouse, parent, child, or close friend. Have you ever felt love and irritation at the same time? Give three examples of the situation and how you handled it. Write in your notebook.

Are you satisfied with the way you handle conflicting emotions? If not, how can you improve the way you handle this situation?

If you think over the times your emotions got the better of you, you will probably notice that the source of your emotional difficulty was two conflicting emotions. The ability to recognize your emotions at the time they occur, to label them and deal with the emotions is the art of sober, well-balanced living.

Actions for the Day (Dinner)

I   Do sixty minutes of reading about sober living. Write down what you got out of the reading, and how it applies to you.

II Attend an A.A. meeting. Be sure to speak at the meeting.

III Call one of the following people: spouse, best friend, parent or sponsor and share with that person how you plan to deal with your feelings more effectively. Be open and honest in this conversation. Share your feelings with the person you are calling.

IV Write down the reactions and the impressions of the person you called.

Feelings: Review of the Day (Beverage Break)

I   Practice the art of giving. Giving does not necessarily mean that you give an object. You can give yourself. Give to another person.

II What did you give? To whom? How do you feel about giving? Write it down.

III If you feel that you have successfully completed this day, that you have worked at your sober living and that you are better in touch with your feelings, give yourself a pat on the back. Enjoy your success.

Daily Reading (While getting ready for bed)

Love

If there is one feeling that alcoholism distorts, it is love. Alcoholics become so wrapped up in themselves, their problems and their maudlin feelings, that love dissipates. You cannot love when the bottle stands in the way.

Love is what you make it. If you are getting drunk, all the energy you spend on getting drunk is in the way of love. All the guilt and remorse you have between drunks gets in the way of love.

The alcoholic is on a love roller coaster. There are moments of independence and arrogance. There are times of maudlin, tearful dependence. These sharp swings in affection get in the way of love. The alcoholic cannot realize love again until he sobers up and begins practicing sober living. The alcoholic, when sober, needs to review his relationship with those he loves. This is not easy because it means talking to the individual you love and reviewing that love. Men, especially, are very threatened by this. They feel uncomfortable talking about love, especially with the one they love.

How can you do this? How can you review with the one you love the condition of the relationship? First, you do it when the two of you are alone. Second, you wait until you have at least two weeks of sober living behind you. Third, you say to the person, "Do you know that I love you?" This is the hard part because many people wonder what they will say next. The next step is to simply continue the conversation. Be honest yet be succinct. Remember, the other person may also feel awkward.

Alcoholics become so wrapped up in their drinking and troubles that they lose contact with the people they love. Now that you have begun sober living, you can no longer take love for granted. Love is a feeling, a good feeling, a secure feeling. The more you share this feeling with those you love, even though you may feel uncomfortable, the more you will love.

Reading Review

In two or three sentences, describe the point of today's reading.

How does today's reading pertain to you? Give at least two examples.

Can you implement in your life something from today's reading? Write down how you can implement today's reading in your life.

Evening Reflection (When in bed)

The entire day was spent on feelings, specifically the feelings of giving and love. End the day by reflecting on what you have learned. What new meaning does love have for you? How do you plan to practice love? Love is the greatest human emotion because it allows us to rise above ourselves.

Day Twenty—*You Can't Get Drunk If You Don't Have The First One . . .*

Morning Meditation (Upon Rising)

Communicate with your Higher Power. Lift your spirit beyond yourself. If the weather permits, do your morning meditation outside. See the beauty and greatness of the world and then relate the world around you to the whole universe. Think about the creator of this universe. Don't bog yourself down with theological or religious principle. Let your spirit communicate with your Higher Power.

Thinking About Yourself (Breakfast)

Sober living is the healthy combination of biology, psychology, sociology, and spirituality. We take care of our body, our mind, our family, and our friends.

Many people stop at this point, they do not complete themselves. Each person, in order to feel complete and whole, needs to understand himself or herself as a spiritual being. Not that we need a specific religion or God (though these are helpful to many), but we need to be in touch with ourselves and our universe.

Each person practicing sober living needs a healthy spiritual life. What is your spiritual life? Be specific. Identify your spiritual beliefs and practices. Write in your notebook.

Are you satisfied with your spiritual life? If so, write down why you are satisfied. If not, write down what you can do to satisfy your need for a healthy spiritual life.

How can you improve the quality of your spiritual life? Are you living in accord with the practices of your personal spirituality? If so, can you intensify this experience? If not, do you want to identify yourself with an organized religion? How can you do this?

Emotional Growth (Lunch)

Sober living is a mixture of independence and dependence. Independence from the sedative chemical alcohol and dependence upon self. Sober living also means dependence upon others for support and assistance. It is a recognition of our dependence upon a Higher Power. Without this recognition, our world and our place in the world are incomplete. Some recovering alcoholics have difficulty coming to grips with the concept of a Higher Power. Frequently, the difficulty is an intellectual dilemma. Sometimes, it is pride and arrogance. It may also be emotional resistance to a position of dependence. How does the concept of a Higher Power effect you emotionally? Write your answer.

Describe how you plan to continue emotional growth within yourself, between yourself and others and between yourself and your Higher Power.

Sober Life-Style (Coffee Break)

For many recovering alcoholics church is a difficult thought. Many of these individuals stopped the practices of their church. Others never really had the practice of church attendance. Is there room for church in your life? If so, describe what the practice will be. If not, what are your specific plans in the area of spiritual growth and development? Write in your notebook.

Within each of us there is a need for ritual and cultural traditions. For many of us church provides the ritual in our lives. Even though costumes, music and ritualistic behavior patterns may make us feel uncomfortable, we have a psychological need for them. If you enjoy these customs and go to church regularly you are fortunate. What do you get out of church attendance? Do you contribute money? If you are uncomfortable going to church, how will you deal with your need for ritual? Does this decision have an effect on you? How about your spouse or family? Even if you choose not to go to church there are other ways to partake in the rites of the culture. How can you do this? Be specific in your written answers.

Actions for the Day (Dinner)

I   Take time to perform some action related to your spiritual life.

II Attend an A.A. meeting. If possible, talk about the role of your spiritual life and how it enhances your sober living. If you don't get a chance to talk during the meeting, find someone after the meeting and share with that person something about your spiritual life.

III Do something to make yourself feel good. What did you do? Why did it make you feel good?

IV Do something to make another person feel good. What did you do? How did it make them feel? How did it make you feel? Describe the activity.

Feelings: Review of the Day (Beverage Break)

I Do something (thought or action) that will make you feel closer to your Higher Power.

II After you've done this, write down how you felt about communicating with your Higher Power. Be open and honest in this paragraph.

III Practice feeling good.

IV Practice relaxation exercises.

V Practice feeling accomplished.

Daily Reading (While getting ready for bed)

Sober Living When You Are Nervous

Who hasn't been nervous at some time or other? Nervousness consumes great amounts of energy. Nervousness takes time. Nervousness is a drag, a real impediment to successful sober living. But we all get nervous from time to time. Some of us get nervous more often than others.

Nervousness is a psychological state. We know we are nervous because there is a sinking feeling in our stomach, the palms of our hands get moist, we perspire, we get restless, we pace, we fret, we worry, we're on edge, we can't sit still, we can't concentrate, we may feel frightened, we may feel apprehensive, we may anticipate something terrible. Nervousness consumes a great deal of psychological energy in a nonproductive, repetitive fashion.

When do you get nervous? Some people get nervous in specific situations, others are nervous all the time. Understanding what makes us nervous does not always reduce the anxiety, but frequently allows us to better cope with it. Sometimes we become nervous for reasons that are valid. However, most of the time we become nervous for invalid, silly reasons.

Most people react to nervous days in ways that make them even more nervous. Worry leads to more worry. Fear creates fear. Anxiety builds upon anxiety. We create our own problems when we worry. Worry is a waste of time. It is self-destructive. But none of these explanations or interpretations help when we're nervous. Understanding nervousness won't help us to solve the problem, but it will allow us to take steps toward removing the nervousness.

Anxiety is either rational or irrational. Rational anxiety is based upon reality. A soldier going into combat experiences rational anxiety. Something dreadful could happen to that soldier. However, most nervousness is irrational. Irrational anxiety tends to be vague. Vague nervousness is irrational and one can often dispel it by laughing at oneself for being nervous over something so silly or far-fetched. If irrational anxiety persists, seek professional help.

Some people believe their anxiety is due to constitutional factors. They like to convince themselves they have weaknesses or they have a nervous problem. These people are looking for excuses to avoid doing something about their irrational fears and anxieties. Even people who are in the weakest physical condition can get rid of irrational fears and anxieties if they want to. But some people don't want to stop being nervous. These people get something out of nervousness. What they get from nervousness is the ability to avoid what they do not like or do not want to do. "I'm too nervous to do it," they say. If you want to avoid being emotionally crippled by anxiety you must be willing to do whatever is necessary to overcome anxiety.

For some people, nervousness is a way to get pills. They take pills to deal with their anxiety rather than learning to solve the problem. They choose to become dependent upon tranquilizers rather than develop the skill of solving problems that make them nervous. The alcoholic needs to be particularly careful of this pitfall. Many alcoholics used drinking as a way to deal with their anxiety. Once they sober up, some alcoholics use pills instead of alcohol. They miss the whole point. They avoid developing skills to combat anxiety. Instead, they choose to stay chemically dependent.

The solution to nervousness is relaxation. Some people try to achieve relaxation by seeking instant temporary relief in a pill. But the pill or chemical gives only limited relief, requires increasing dosages for the same amount of relief and impairs other functions of normal life.

Relaxation training is a better way to develop the relaxation response. Relaxation training is taught in this book. There are also several fine books on the market that teach relaxation. If you are the nervous type, learn how to relax.

Overcoming nervousness requires action. Ordinarily, the last thing a nervous person wants to do is take action. However, there are certain steps that must be taken in order to deal effectively with nervousness. These steps are designed to reduce the anxiety, not to ignore it or increase it.

The first step is to recognize the nervousness. Say to yourself, "I am nervous."

The second step is to identify what is making you nervous. "I am nervous because I am going to the dentist."

The third step is to discover if the nervousness is rational or irrational. If it is rational, grin and bear it (but continue to the next step). If it is irrational (as most anxiety is), say to yourself, "This is silly and irrational nervousness."

The fourth step is to perform a task that will reduce the nervousness. Action reduces anxiety. Do what has to be done. If nothing needs to be done, do a chore or job that will keep you busy until the anxiety is reduced.

The fifth step is to practice your relaxation exercises.

The sixth step is to think about what you have just learned from the experience of nervousness and how you can improve the situation in the future.

We all get nervous from time to time. Do not let anxiety get in the way of successful living. The ability to realize that most anxiety is irrational and silly helps us to get into action. Taking action gives us something to do about our nervousness besides worrying about it.

Practice relaxing. Learn to deal with your nervousness in a problem solving fashion.

Reading Review

In two or three sentences, describe the point of today's reading.

How does today's reading pertain to you? Give at least two examples.

Can you implement in your life something from today's reading? Write down how you can implement today's reading in your life.

Evening Reflection (When in bed)

Contemplate the following A.A. prayer:
"God grant me the Serenity to accept
   the things I cannot change,
Courage to change the things I can,
And Wisdom to know the difference."

Day Twenty-One—*Principles Before Personalities . . .*

Morning Meditation (Upon Rising)

> God grant me the Serenity to accept
>   the things I cannot change,
> Courage to change the things I can,
> And Wisdom to know the difference.

Read this thought two or three times. As you do so, think of the application of this prayer to your life. Mentally picture yourself applying this to your life. Spend fifteen minutes in meditation.

Thinking About Yourself (Breakfast)

As you come to the end of your third week, it is good to review what you've accomplished so far. If you have completed all the assignments you have been given, you have accomplished the following essential actions toward sober living:

1. Admitted you are an alcoholic by taking Step One of A.A.
2. Became an active, practicing member of A.A.
3. Had a spiritual awakening through Steps Two and Three of A.A.
4. Developed a foundation of honesty by practicing the truth.
5. Taken the Fourth and Fifth Steps of A.A.
6. Found an A.A. sponsor and possible A.A. home group.
7. Identified major problems and implemented a problem solving way of life.
8. Learned about impulses to drink and how to deal with them.
9. Dealt with your character defects and shortcomings through Steps Six and Seven of A.A.
10. Developed a sober living schedule that is well-balanced.
11. Learned how feelings affect your sober living and developed effective ways for dealing with feelings.
12. Made a list of people you had harmed and made amends where possible through taking Steps Eight and Nine of A.A.
13. Felt good about yourself and what you are doing.

Review each of these actions you have taken over the past few weeks.

1. Admitted you are an alcoholic by taking Step One of A.A. Why did you do it? How will it affect your sober living? How do you feel about it? Write in your notebook.

2. Became an active, practicing member of A.A. Why did you do it? How will it affect your sober living? How do you feel about it?

3. Had a spiritual awakening through Steps Two and Three of A.A. Describe the awakening. How does this pertain to your sober living?

4. Developed a foundation of honesty by practicing the truth. Why did you do it? How will it affect your sober living?

5. Took the Fourth and Fifth Steps of A.A. Why did you do it? How will it affect your sober living? How do you feel about it?

6. Found an A.A. sponsor and possible A.A. home group. Why did you do it? How will it affect your sober living? How do you feel about it?

7. Identified major problems in your life and implemented a problem solving way of life. Why did you do it? How will it affect your sober living? How do you feel about it?

8. Learned about impulses to drink and discovered a way to deal with them. Why did you do it? How will it affect your sober living? How do you feel about it?

9. Dealt with your character defects and shortcomings through Steps Six and Seven of A.A. How did you do this? What affect does this have on your sober living?

10. Developed a sober living schedule that is well-balanced. Why did you do it? How will it affect your sober living? How do you feel about it?

11. Learned how feelings affect your sober living and developed effective ways for dealing with feelings. Why did you do it? How will it affect your sober living? How do you feel about it?

12. Made a list of people you had harmed and made amends when possible after taking Steps Eight and Nine of A.A. Describe how you did this, how you felt about it and how these two A.A. steps will affect your sober living.

13. Felt good about yourself and what you were doing. Why

did you do it? How will it affect your sober living? How do you feel about it?

Emotional Growth (Lunch)

You have taken important strides toward sober living. The recovering alcoholic who is progressing nicely towards sober living often has a nagging doubt, a continuing fear of failure. This is a normal reaction. This is probably not the first time you have tried to quit drinking alcoholic beverages. Usually there has been an experience of failure for anyone who has progressed as far as you have. Identify your concerns about failure. Don't panic. Realize that success is in your hands. Sober living is yours for the taking.

Do you have any nagging doubts about failure to achieve sober living? What are they? Be specific. If you don't, do you think you are over-confident? Write your answers in your notebook.

How do you plan to deal with your feelings of possible failure or success?

Many recovering alcoholics deal with feelings of possible failure or success by sharing them with their A.A. sponsor or someone close who is involved in their recovery. Is there someone you can share this feeling with?

Sober Life-Style (Coffee Break)

The sober living plan is more than a paper exercise. It is best to look at it every morning after meditation. It is important to have a plan of activities and events for each day. The sober living schedule is flexible enough to meet the variable demands of each day, and structured enough to help us do each day everything we must do to keep sober.

There will be a tendency to slide away from the daily use of the sober living schedule. A sense of self-control may urge you to feel you don't need to review your sober living schedule. Pride may take over, or a false belief that you have everything under control. You may think you no longer need the structure of a daily schedule.

Resist these impulses. Develop the habit, each morning after your morning meditation, of organizing your day and reviewing your sober living schedule. Do you look at your schedule every morning after meditation? What value do you see in using a daily sober living schedule? Write your answers.

Is there anything you can do to increase the value derived from the use of the sober living schedule? If so, describe it. If not, why not?

How do you plan to ensure that you review your schedule daily? Be specific and detailed.

Actions for the Day (Dinner)

I   Find a person to whom you feel close and share with this person how you feel about your progress. Mention your specific progress on each of the steps you've taken toward sober living.

II   Go to an A.A. meeting.

III Do something of a recreational nature to reward yourself for a good week.

Feelings: Review of the Day (Beverage Break)

Write down how you *feel* about yourself three weeks later.

I   Practice feeling good.

II   Practice feeling relaxed.

III Practice feeling accomplished.

Daily Reading (While getting ready for bed)

Review and Preview

Marvin Hamlisch wrote a song called, "Memories." It is a plaintive and haunting melody. The essential theme of the song is that memories may be beautiful because we tend to forget painful memories. This seems to be a common phenomenon. We tend to embellish and romanticize pleasant memories and minimize or forget unpleasant memories. This could be disastrous for the alcoholic. The alcoholic usually decides to practice sober living because life as a practicing alcoholic has become too uncomfortable or painful. Objective recollection of what drinking has done to our lives keeps us sober. There may be some discomfort in remembering. You may experience feelings of guilt, embarrassment or shame, but if you forget or minimize what drinking has done to you, you run the risk of returning to drinking.

There is no need to lie to yourself. Of course there are fond memories of incidences that occurred while drinking. There is no value in saying to yourself that all of your drinking activities were painful. There were fun times when you were drinking. But keep in mind your original motives for sobering up—the reasons that forced you to begin to practice sober living.

The present and future are rooted in the past. In order to be what you want to be, it is good to keep an eye on where you have come from. You caused yourself sufficient discomfort by excessive alcohol ingestion to decide to quit drinking. What we recommend is that you periodically and systematically recall to yourself what drinking did to your life and others around you. Life review can revitalize your motives for the continued practice of sober living.

Many people use their A.A. participation to review their lives. This may be a beneficial exercise. The drunkalogue which we discussed before allows some individuals to remember the past. It enables them to keep the past sufficiently in mind while they focus on living soberly in the present.

There are, however, two traps with the drunkalogue. The first is that the individual repeats the same story so many times that it loses its value. The story becomes desensitized. That is, it loses its value to emotionally remind the person of the discomfort that forced him to sober up. Another variant on this first trap is that we begin to tell the story more for the audience than for ourselves. Or we begin to embellish the story with exaggerations and lies. What began as one case of beer and a speeding ticket, can become two cases of beer and a week in jail if we are not careful.

The second trap with the drunkalogue is that it can become automatic and machine-like, a tape recording of the past events of someone else. In other words, the drunkalogue can become depersonalized. It can become a story about some-body else, a piece of good fiction, but not about you.

The drunkalogue is good for the practice of sober living. However, we need to practice honesty and humility in our drunkalogues. Try to recall different stories. Sometimes emphasize what you did to others. Sometimes focus on what drinking did to your emotions, to your integrity and to your health. Point out to your listener how you benefit from sharing your drunkalogue. If you can't feel how you personally benefit from the drunkalogue, then you are entertaining the folks, you are on an ego trip or just passing the time with a good story.

Another review of the past that helps to keep motivation well tuned is continued use of the Fourth and Fifth Steps on a periodic and systematic basis. Monthly use of the Fourth and Fifth Steps allows us to review our progress in sober living. We will talk about the Tenth Step at a later date.

Review is only good if it helps us live in the present in a productive and happy fashion. Preview, on the other hand, allows us to prepare for the future. It enables us to live tomorrow in a better way. Review focuses upon who you are. Where you came from. What you did. Preview looks at where you want to go. How you want to live. Preview is an act of planning or goal setting.

Goal setting is the ability to define where you want to be at a certain point in your life. Good goal setting is time specific. For example, "In two years I intend to have enough money saved for a down payment on a house." Planning is setting up the steps and actions necessary to achieve the goal.

Previewing your life is nothing more than setting some goals for yourself and developing the plans to achieve these goals. There are a few guidelines to follow when previewing. First of all, always set realistic goals. Some individuals are inclined to be overly optimistic. They set goals which in all probability they will never realistically accomplish, like becoming a millionaire or a president of the company. Set realistic goals. Prepare yourself to win. If you set goals that are virtually impossible to accomplish, you will probably lose.

The second step in goal setting is to set different kinds of goals. In terms of time, set only one or two long-term goals (goals that will take more than a year to accomplish). Set one or two intermediate goals (goals that will take more than a month). Set one or two short-term goals (goals that you can accomplish in a week or less).

Do not make all your goals of an acquisitive nature or of an avoidance nature. Be realistic and vary them. Set goals that will allow you to acquire items or skills which you want to acquire, like a new house, or the skill of being charitable or telling the truth. Set some avoidance goals. For example, avoiding resentments, avoiding lying or avoiding being late for work.

Planning is the second step of previewing. After setting goals, we need a set of steps that will lead to accomplishment of the goals. Goals need to be realistic and so do plans. We cannot proceed too quickly or we are likely to tire of the pace. We should not proceed too slowly, or we may become bored or tired of repetition.

Plans should be specific. When are you going to do it? How are you going to do it? How will you know you have done it?

Finally, as you accomplish different steps or goals, reward yourself. Be good to yourself. Praise yourself. On the other hand, if you fall behind in your plans or don't accomplish your goals, don't reward yourself. Take your goals seriously and deny yourself some reward or indulgence if you fail to accomplish them. Set new plans and use the past failure to revitalize your plans and goals.

Successful living does not happen accidentally. It is based on the systematic review and preview of life. If the recovering alcoholic develops the habit of periodically reviewing and previewing life, the chances of successful, happy living are increased.

Reading Review

In two or three sentences, describe the point of today's reading.

How does today's reading pertain to you? Give at least two examples.

Can you implement in your life something from today's reading? Write down how you can implement today's reading in your life.

Evening Reflection (When in bed)

Spend a few moments reviewing your life. Attempt to put your life into a real perspective. See not only your failures but your successes.

Spend the next few minutes letting your mind see yourself in the future. See yourself as a successful, sober person. Picture yourself as a sober, working, happy and successful person.

Finally, spend two or three minutes feeling gratitude for all of the good in your life. Be grateful to your Higher Power for your life successes so far. Revitalize your commitment to a lifetime of sober living.

Prologue to Week Four

Self-discipline is the backbone of sober living. It was through self-indulgence, giving in to ourselves, being easy on ourselves, taking the easy way out, that we slowly eroded our lives. Sober living cannot long tolerate corner cutting.

Self-discipline is the ability to do something regularly, regardless of how you feel. It is the ability to do something because you decided to do it and because you hold yourself responsible to carry out the task. Some days it will be easy. Some days it will be very painful. Some days it will come naturally and you will not even notice it.

Self-discipline will support your sober living on days when you do not feel like staying sober, or on days when you think you can have just one drink. Those days will come. *They will.* They will come more than once.

Self-discipline requires practice. As you daily practice your sober living plan through this workbook, your self-discipline is strengthening. Self-discipline is strengthened and reinforced by practice and habit. By establishing the habit of doing what you need to do everyday to maintain sober living, you are building sober living. Practice sober living everyday with all the intensity and zeal you can conjure up, and you will be developing self-discipline.

Remember, it will be self-discipline that will allow you to continue practicing sober living when every fibre in your body says, "Have a drink." Self-discipline is acquired by doing every day what you have to do. Self-discipline is the habit of doing what you set out to do.

During this fourth week of recovery we will focus upon self-discipline, the skills and inner resources that will keep you sober. A.A. Steps Ten, Eleven, and Twelve have a special value in maintaining sobriety. They are self-discipline in action.

Step 10—"Continued to take personal inventory and when we were wrong promptly admitted it."

Step 11—"Sought through prayer and meditation to improve our conscious contact with God *as we understood Him*, praying only for knowledge of His will for us and the power to carry that out."

Step 12—"Having had a spiritual awakening as the result of these steps, we tried to carry this message to alcoholics, and to practice these principles in all our affairs."

It is the practice of Steps Ten, Eleven and Twelve with regularity and consistency that will allow the other A.A. Steps to pervade our lives with sobriety. Sobriety turns into sober living when we discipline ourselves to practice it with daily regularity.

Your A.A. Program so far:

1) "We admitted we were powerless over alcohol—that our lives had become unmanageable."
2) "Came to believe that a Power greater than ourselves could restore us to sanity."
3) "Made a decision to turn our will and our lives over to the care of God *as we understood him.*"
4) "Made a searching and fearless moral inventory of ourselves."
5) "Admitted to God, to ourselves, and to another human being the exact nature of our wrongs."
6) "Were entirely ready to have God remove all these defects of character."
7) "Humbly asked Him to remove our shortcomings."
8) "Made a list of all persons we had harmed, and became willing to make amends to them all."
9) "Made direct amends to such people wherever possible, except when to do so would injure them or others."

Day Twenty-Two—*One Day at a Time . . .*

Morning Meditation (Upon Rising)

Sober living is well-balanced. Sober living is thinking, feeling, and acting in ways that strengthen sobriety. To live soberly you must do things that enhance sober living. You must think about things in a problem solving way. You must express feelings in ways that are healthy. Step Ten of A.A. says, "Continued to take personal inventory and when we were wrong promptly admitted it." In Week Two you took your Fourth and Fifth Steps. At that time you learned that there is no such thing as a perfect Fourth or Fifth Step. The intent of Step Ten is to periodically review your life, your progress and your sober living.

Only God is without error. As humans we make mistakes even when we are trying to be as sober, honest and well-motivated as possible. Because of our human frailty, there is always room for constant review and challenge. Many recovering alcoholics review the Tenth Step once a week, usually at the end of the week. This allows the individual to review the week and to set goals for the coming week.

The Tenth Step should be an exercise in total honesty. When there is accomplishment, praise yourself. If there are shortcomings or failures, identify them. Make plans to improve the weak areas and set new goals to solve each problem.

Thinking About Yourself (Breakfast)

Recovering from alcoholism means changing your thinking, especially your thinking about yourself. What are your thoughts about yourself? How have they improved? How do your thoughts about yourself affect the way you live? Write in your notebook.

Sober living has become your dominant thought and goal. What other goals do you have for yourself? List at least three other significant goals.

What will you do when a problem arises that obstructs the achievement of your goals? Be specific in your answer. Think ahead about future problem areas. What kind of problem can get in the way of your goals? What is your plan of action to overcome this kind of problem?

Emotional Growth (Lunch)

Are there specific feelings that you are still concerned about? What are those feelings? How do you intend to deal with them?

Alcohol used to interact with your feelings in different ways. Alcohol may have enhanced your feelings. It may have helped you dull your feelings. It may have allowed you to feel. Now that drinking alcoholic beverages is no longer a part of your life-style, your feelings will stand naked. How do you feel about expressing your feelings without the use of alcohol?

Do you feel ready to deal with your feelings without alcohol? If so, why, and how will you do it? If not, why not, and what are you going to do about it?

How do you feel about yourself today in comparison to how you felt about yourself before you started this workbook? Be specific. Give examples if you can.

Do you feel that you are in touch with your emotions? How? What does being in touch with your emotions mean to you?

Sober Life-Style (Coffee Break)

Now that you're practicing sober living instead of drinking, what are you doing differently? Be specific. Write in your notebook.

Review in your mind the basic concept of the problem solving life-style. If you don't remember it, go back and review. What is your plan to solve problems as they arise in your life? How will you keep yourself a problem solving, growing individual?

How is your thinking different now than it was before you started this workbook? How do you think differently about others, work, sober living and other important issues?

The Tenth Step begins a style of thinking that periodically reviews our behavior. It allows us to correct our errors and to renew our daily goal of sober living. How do you intend to use the Tenth Step of A.A.? When? Where?

What do you expect to achieve by taking the Tenth Step regularly?

Have you included a periodic personal inventory in your sober living schedule? If not, do it. Plan to take the Tenth Step weekly. The end of the week is the best time for this activity.

How will you be able to carry out your sober living plan without the use of alcohol? Be specific. Review your plan. Give examples.

Actions for the Day (Dinner)

I   Go to an A.A. meeting.

II   Share with someone at the A.A. meeting how you feel about continuing to take personal inventory.

III Make someone happy. What did you do? Write your answer in your notebook.

Feelings: Review of the Day (Beverage Break)

I   Make yourself happy. What did you do to make yourself happy? Write in your notebook.

II   Call the person you called on Day One to tell them you were recovering from alcoholism. In this call, tell the same person how you feel about recovery and independent, sober living. Write down your reactions to this phone call. How do you feel? How does this person you telephoned feel about you?

III Practice relaxation training once today. If you don't remember how to do it, review that section of the book. Go through all the muscles. Relax each set of muscles in a systematic fashion. Do this in a quiet place, preferably while in bed waiting for sleep.

Daily Reading (While getting ready for bed)

Building For A Drunk

Around Alcoholics Anonymous you hear a lot of talk about dry drunks. Dry drunks, the A.A. old-timers will tell you, occur with predictable regularity. Some old-timers even predict that they happen on the fifth day, fifth week and fifth month. Some say the third day, third week and third month. Their predictions may vary, but these successful A.A. members are trying to tell you that there are periods when you are vulnerable to a return to drinking.

The phrase "building for a drunk" implies that the recovering alcoholic who returns to drinking does not do so without warning. Some alcoholics return to drinking on an impulse and with no warning, but in most instances there are little telltale signs that the sober living has begun to erode. The phrase "building for a drunk" describes it well because it usually starts with small, virtually unnoticed changes. These changes gain momentum. As they pick up strength the new sober living habits fade away until there is a return to drinking.

Building for a drunk means a change in your life-style. This is a change in your sober living plan that has not been discussed with some other person, a spouse, an A.A. sponsor, your alcoholism counselor. Frequently, the recovering alcoholic is unaware of the change. However, when the change is brought to his or her attention, he or she becomes quite defensive.

For example, an individual whose sober living schedule called for three A.A. meetings per week finds that the one on Friday nights prevents her from joining a bowling league. Instead of discussing this with someone who is knowledgeable about alcoholism and her specific problem, she independently decides to drop the Friday night A.A. meeting for Friday night bowling. After a couple of weeks, the husband becomes aware of this change. He discusses it with her, and instead of a logical discussion and an awareness that the change is eroding her sober living, she becomes defensive and finds fault with her husband. She feels he doesn't trust her, although she feels she has it all under control. The fact is, this individual is building for a drunk. Not because she went to bowling instead of A.A., but because she defensively refuses to review her sober living plan. She avoided checking with someone before she changed, and now she won't recognize that she is setting herself up for a return to drinking.

There will be times when everything goes wrong, you'll be under pressure and you'll want to cut back on your sober living plans. It may even be reasonable to reduce some of your activities. Only do this with the advice of someone who is close to you, preferably your counselor.

Mood is another aspect of building for a drunk. We all have good days and bad days. However, if we find ourselves in a bad mood, irritable, tired, or cranky, we may be building for a drunk. An extra A.A. meeting can be helpful when moodiness is a problem. It may help to review your honesty. Are you being totally honest with yourself?

Any change in activity, mood, or personality can be an indication that you are building for a drunk. What do you do? First, discuss it with another person. Second, revitalize your sober living plan, get active and go to an extra A.A. meeting. It is wise at the A.A. meeting to mention that you are having difficulty. Be humble enough to follow the advice you receive. Be honest with yourself.

Reading Review

In two or three sentences, describe the point of today's reading.

How does today's reading pertain to you? Give at least two examples.

Can you implement in your life something from today's reading? Write down how you can implement today's reading in your life.

Evening Reflection (When in bed)

I am sober. I am a good person. Even though today was not perfect, my intentions were good, and I am sober. How can I live better tomorrow, and improve my sober living?

Day Twenty-Three—Courage To Change The Things I Can . . .

Morning Meditation (Upon Rising)

Drinking isolates the alcoholic. Each recovering alcoholic needs to assess the impact of drinking on family, friends, and acquaintances.

In the area of family, there are two dimensions to be aware of. The first is the feeling of guilt you may experience due to things you did while drinking. The second dimension is the feeling of disappointment different family members may have toward you.

Friends sometimes are more tolerant of our misdeeds than are family members. They often do not express their feelings of disappointment. Instead they drift away from us and have less and less to do with us.

Acquaintances are the least tolerant of the practicing alcoholic. They accept only those interactions and activities they approve of. They are the most likely to strike out and express resentment and anger towards the alcoholic who does something they disapprove of.

Family and friends have a lot to do with sober living. Friends who are mature, responsible adults, who preferably don't drink alcoholic beverages, can strengthen sober living. A close, loving family can also strengthen sober living.

Steps Eight and Nine of A.A. deal directly with our social network. Review in your heart Steps Eight and Nine—"Made a list of all persons we had harmed, and became willing to make amends to them all" and "Made direct amends to such people wherever possible, except when to do so would injure them or others." Keep in mind that just because you are aware of those whom you have hurt or offended, and just because you made amends wherever possible, you cannot expect these people (family and friends), to automatically forgive and forget. Give them time. Give yourself time at sober living. You will find that the daily practice of sober living, as the Twelve Steps of A.A. teach, brings most people around to forgiveness.

Thinking About Yourself (Breakfast)

You will not drink today and you will live the day in the best way you can. How will your sober living affect your family?

What will be different, and what will you do differently with your family?

Remember, different family members will feel differently toward you. Some friends may want nothing to do with you now that you are sober. On the other hand, some friends and family members may be too solicitous, too concerned, even smothering. Whatever their reaction, you have to deal with it. Never forget that these people you love are reacting to a problem you caused. Don't expect miracles. Practice sober living every day and with time the emotional reaction of others toward you will return to normal.

How is your family included in your sober living plans?

Do you intend to keep all the same friends? If so, why and how will this affect your sober living plans? If not, why not and how will this affect your sober living plans?

Emotional Growth (Lunch)

You have been practicing sober living for a few weeks now. Take time to review your emotional development.

The entire thrust of the last seven days of the sober living workbook is putting it all back together. It is the practice of sober living. Take time during the day to get in touch with your feelings and to improve your emotional state.

Many recovering alcoholics who have developed their emotional lives, find time daily to practice relaxation, feeling good and feeling accomplished. It doesn't take long. Your lunch break or after work are good times to do this.

Sitting alone, close your eyes and let a good feeling come over you. Picture yourself on a warm beach feeling good. Tense and relax your muscles. Feel relaxed. Review your accomplishment. You are sober. Your life is improving. Feel accomplished. Do you feel guilty or nervous about past behavior and how it affected your family? If not, why not? Write in your notebook.

How do you intend to express your feelings towards your family? Be specific in your answer.

How do you expect your friends to react to your sober living? Be specific. Mention any difficulties you anticipate.

Sober Life-Style (Coffee Break)

What do you intend to do differently with your friends?

How do your friends fit into your sober living plans? Be specific.

Actions for the Day (Dinner)

I   Go to an A.A. meeting. After the meeting ask someone (one of the old-timers) how family and friends affected their sober living.

II   Write down what you learned in this conversation.

III Call a friend and share with that friend your thoughts and feelings about the future of your new sober life.

IV   Write down the name of the person you called and their reaction to your phone call.

Feelings: Review of the Day (Beverage Break)

How do you feel about completing the workbook?

How do you feel about your friends?

How do you express these feelings?

How do you feel about your family?

How do you express these feelings?

Daily Reading (While getting ready for bed)

Watch Out For The Letdown

In a few days you will complete four weeks of active learning and growing in sober living. There have probably been moments of happiness, well-being and guiltlessness. Only you know how much you have gotten out of the program, and only you know how much you've paid for your successes.

As you prepare to finish the workbook, there is one remaining word of caution. Most people finish the program feeling well. These people usually experience a sense of completion. They are happy. Those around them will feel happy to have them sober. Likewise, work will ordinarily be a positive experience. However, sooner or later, in a few days or perhaps weeks, there may be a letdown.

The letdown will probably be unnoticed at first. Gradually you will become aware that life goes on. Day in and day out, it is up to you to practice sober living. The most difficult part is the realization that most people expect you to live and function maturely, soberly and productively. There are no brass bands for doing what is normal. This causes problems for some recovering alcoholics. They want more. They want recognition. However, you won't get recognition for doing what you're supposed to do, for what everybody else does without any applause.

This is the test of sober living. Sober living is fine as long as you are feeling happy and getting recognition. It's a different story when you do it for yourself no matter how you feel. Sober living is expected. It is the foundation for all that you can do. If you need recognition, then go out and do something worthy of recognition.

When you are feeling down because the halo effect has worn off, it is time to reassess your motives. Remember, you chose sober living because you were unhappy with the way you were living. You chose it for yourself. You were the one who wanted it. You have it. You alone can keep it.

How do you remotivate yourself when it doesn't seem worth it? You keep doing what your sober living plan calls for. No matter how bad it gets, it can get worse if you return to drinking. Remind yourself of how things were when you were drinking.

The letdown will easily be put into perspective if we have a healthy view of reality. Letdowns occur more frequently for those individuals who overinflate their own sense of worth. Step Eleven of Alcoholics Anonymous says—"Sought through prayer and meditation to improve our conscious contact with God *as we understood Him,* praying only for knowledge of His will for us and the power to carry that out." The letdown can be avoided, not by praying to avoid it, but by praying for knowledge of God's will and strength.

The Eleventh Step is a spiritual growth step. Practice of this step allows us to keep our sober living on an even keel. Many recovering alcoholics resist this step. These same individuals have difficulty finding inner peace with their sobriety. Practice of the Eleventh Step develops the inner strength and peace that makes a sober life worth living.

Reading Review

In two or three sentences, describe the point of today's reading.

How does today's reading pertain to you? Give at least two examples.

Can you implement in your life something from today's reading? Write down how you can implement today's reading in your life.

Evening Reflection (When in bed)

"God grant me the Serenity to accept
  the things I cannot change,
Courage to change the things I can,
And Wisdom to know the difference."

Ponder this A.A. thought. How can you apply it to your life?

Day Twenty-Four—*Wisdom to Know the Difference . . .*

Morning Meditation (Upon Rising)

There's an old saying which reads, "If you can't give it, you ain't got it." There is a lot of truth in this saying, especially for someone recovering from alcoholism. Giving your help to others is a good way to strengthen your own sober living. It doesn't have to be fancy or exotic giving. Start by cleaning up the ash trays and straightening up the room after an A.A. meeting. You may try offering somebody a lift home or picking them up for an A.A. meeting if they have no car. It is better to give somebody a ride home than it is to give them a sermon on the virtues of sobriety.

Spend a few minutes alone and meditate on the thought of giving yourself to others in a productive, happy fashion. How can you make other people happy? What can you offer? Giving yourself and your time may be the best gift you can give.

Thinking About Yourself (Breakfast)

Step Twelve of A.A. reads—"Having had a spiritual awakening as the result of these steps, we tried to carry this message to alcoholics and to practice these principles in all our affairs."

What does this mean to you? Be specific. Write in your notebook.

How do you plan to implement Step Twelve of A.A. in your life? Be specific. Give examples and a possible time-table for implementation.

Emotional Growth (Lunch)

Sometimes people recovering from alcoholism feel overwhelmed by what they consider a loss of personal control over their lives. They feel resentment. They don't want to give up the personal freedom of deciding when to do something. They dislike being tied down to so many A.A. meetings.

Do you feel that you have lost some control of your life since starting treatment for your alcoholism? If so, how? If not, why not? Write in your notebook.

How will you deal with this control issue? Are you in control of your life? Do you choose to recover from alcoholism, choose to develop a sober living plan and choose to go to A.A.?

Are you ready for full control of your life, or do you need some outside help and assistance?

Sober Life-Style (Coffee Break)

Let's review the role of A.A. in your sober living.

1. What is the role of A.A. in your life? Write in your notebook.

2. Do you have an A.A. sponsor? If so, how does that A.A. sponsor function in your life? How often will you meet with your A.A. sponsor? What will you do or discuss with your A.A. sponsor?

3. Do you have an A.A. home group? What is the purpose of an A.A. home group? When will you go there? Will you give anything to the A.A. home group?

4. When do you plan to attend A.A.? Be specific, what meetings, where and when?

5. Develop a Step Twelve plan. Be specific. Twelfth Step activities include bringing the message of hope and recovery to practicing alcoholics. How will you do this? Be specific. Some A.A. groups have hot-lines or crisis numbers. You could volunteer your time. Some communities have A.A. inter-groups that have a wide variety of Step Twelve activities. Alcohol treatment programs need volunteers. What is your Step Twelve plan?

6. Do you intend to read A.A. material? Be specific.

Actions for the Day (Dinner)

I   Review your sober living plan. See that it is consistent with all you've said today about participation in A.A. Have you scheduled specific time for A.A. activities?

II   Attend an A.A. meeting. After the meeting, talk to someone about your A.A. plans. What did that person think of your A.A. plans?

Feelings: Review of the Day (Beverage Break)

I   How do you feel about A.A.? Be specific. Practice honesty.

II   Do you ever get bored at an A.A. meeting? If so, what do you do about it? If not, why not?

III   What do you do when you don't feel like going to an A.A. meeting, yet your sober living plan calls for an A.A. meeting? How will you discipline yourself concerning your A.A. needs?

IV   Practice feeling wholesome. Do something to make another person feel worthwhile and wholesome.

V   What did you do?

Daily Reading (While getting ready for bed)

Sex And Sober Living

Well-balanced living includes some degree of sexual activity for most people. Many people who are recovering from alcoholism have no problem adjusting to a healthy sex life. Some recovering alcoholics have problems with achieving a successful sex life.

What is a successful sex life? There is no single answer to this question. For some people a successful sex life will mean no sex at all, for others it will mean a very active sex life. In other words, the answer is very personal and very private. You cannot read a book and find the ideal sex life for you.

Like most aspects of sober living, arriving at a well-adjusted sex life requires thought and planning. The thinking should start with values. What role does sex play in your sense of moral, spiritual and personal values? This means establishing the rules of the game for you. For example, what are your opinions and attitudes about masturbation, cheating on a spouse, one night stands, and other sexual questions? Each person, in order to have an adjusted pleasurable sex life, needs to have a personal code of sexual conduct. Leave room for creativity and spontaneity, but develop the rules of the game. You will find three common sexual codes in the next paragraphs.

Person A believes that sex is a good interpersonal response to be shared only with the spouse. This person did not engage in intercourse until after marriage. This code of sexual conduct is based on religious principles which condemn masturbation, infidelity and lust. This code allows the individual to relate to the spouse in a creative and personal way. The couple has an active and intense sex life. They talk about their sex life openly and experiment with new positions. They both work on making their sex life exciting and rewarding through open and personal discussion.

Person B is uptight about sex and has poorly defined sexual codes. This person is married and has a rather routine sex life with the spouse. Because of sexual hang-ups, the couple does not talk of ways to improve their sex life. It seems that this person has vague dirty feelings about sex. Likewise, the area of fidelity is vague. This person believes that it is wrong to cheat on the spouse but this person has no specific and personalized reasons for this belief. There have been times, when the occasion arose, that there was sexual infidelity with subsequent guilt feelings. This person is unhappy and unfulfilled in the sexual area and seems to go through life in a repetitive, dull fashion with periodic fantasies of a better sex life. These fantasies are sometimes carried out, but there are always guilt feelings afterwards.

Person C has no personal values about sex other than to do what strikes the fancy. This person is married. The sex life is active, but with less intimacy than this person would desire. Sex is not a pressing issue and this person has sex frequently with many partners. There are no guilt feelings. Life is generally happy and the sex is usually very pleasurable and rewarding. The rule of sexual conduct is enjoyment. This person believes sex is good and the more sex there is the better. The only negative aspect that can be identified is a lack of intimacy and closeness to the marital partner. It seems that sex with other partners, though pleasurable, does keep the couple distant from each other.

These three descriptions are offered as examples, not models. Each person has to develop a personal code of sexual behavior. The only guideline we offer is to develop a code based on personal, ethical and spiritual values. Leave room for intimacy and closeness to the sex partner. Finally, allow sufficient discussion with the partner to develop new and alternate sexual patterns.

Sober living and healthy sexual adjustment go hand in hand. The person practicing sober living has a sex life based on values, not on impulse and whim. This is not to say that a sex life of impulse and whim is wrong, only that a recovering alcoholic functions best when life is structured.

Sexual problems occur under two general conditions. The first is organic; those instances when the body will not perform properly for medical reasons. The second is functional; those instances when the body will not perform for reasons of a psychological nature. Nervousness, depression and exhaustion are examples of psychological causes for sexual problems.

What are some common sexual problems? There are many. The inability to have an orgasm and the inability to achieve erection are two common problems. The inability to relax and enjoy sex without drinking and the inability to have an orgasm or to achieve an erection when drunk are also common. The solution is simple—sober up. Sometimes sexual problems occur after the alcoholic sobers up. These problems are probably caused by guilt or nervousness about sobering up. You will probably get better performance in a few days. Relax, don't rush things.

Problems may occur after you've been sober for a while. Sometimes, in the best of sex lives, a problem can arise that is not related to drinking. Here are a few steps you can take if you find yourself with a sexual problem.

1. Relax. You are probably causing the problem yourself. If the problem is lack of erection or orgasm, you will only increase or exaggerate the problem by thinking about it. You may create a self-fulfilling prophecy with

all your worries. If you are worried that you may not have an erection or an orgasm, you probably won't.

2. Approach sex in your usual way. Be sure to use sufficient foreplay and fantasy. Assist your sexual performance by spicing it with fantasies or images that sexually arouse you.

3. Talk to your sex partner beforehand (if you are close enough that such a discussion does not threaten you). Direct your sex partner to do the things that please you most.

4. Do what turns you on. Prepare yourself to have a successful encounter. Make sure you're in the mood. Do what pleases you.

5. If the sexual problem persists after several attempts, consult your physician. Speak bluntly to the physician about your problem.

There is one additional comment to make on sex and sober living. If you were the kind of person who had to be drunk or drinking to enjoy sex, then you should seek professional help. This is not a big problem, and can be treated easily. Don't pretend it's not a problem. If it is a problem, identify it and do something about it.

Sex and sober living go hand in hand. The practice of sober living includes a well-adjusted, successful sex life. This requires developing a code of sexual conduct by which you can live, and then fulfilling your sexual appetite within this code.

Reading Review

In two or three sentences, describe the point of today's reading.

How does today's reading pertain to you? Give at least two examples.

Can you implement in your life something from today's reading? Write down how you can implement today's reading in your life.

Evening Reflection (When in bed)

Recite the Lord's Prayer to yourself. If you cannot recall the prayer take time to find a book that contains the prayer. Say or read the prayer. Find some line or thought that especially catches your interest and think about the meaning of the words. How can you apply this to your life?

Day Twenty-Five—Let Go and Let God . . .

Morning Meditation (Upon Rising)

As you approach the end of this book think about what you will use in its place. You have been spending a certain amount of time each day developing and improving your life. You have established patterns you will not want to break. The best thing you can do is follow your sober living plan and spend time each day reviewing and previewing your life, always developing, always improving the quality of your life.

The primary focus of this week has been upon independent sober living. Set some specific goals before completing the workbook. Include the following items:

1. Meeting with spouse to review sober living plan and include spouse actively in the sober living plan.
2. Meeting with employer (foreman, supervisor or company alcoholism counselor) to review sober living plan and include employer actively in the sober living plan.
3. Meeting with A.A. sponsor to review sober living plan and include A.A. sponsor in the sober living plan.
4. Meeting with the person who will be your alcoholism counselor to review sober living plan and set up a schedule for aftercare appointments.

Thinking About Yourself (Breakfast)

Let's review your sober living plan. Keep in mind that sober living is well-balanced living. Well-balanced living includes sufficient time for important activities. List the important activities you will include in your plan. When will you perform these activities? Write your answers in your notebook.

Is your sober living plan well-balanced? Describe in detail how you have planned to do all that you need to do. How will you ensure that you will carry out what you've planned?

What are the weak links in your sober living plan, and how do you intend to compensate for these weaknesses? Be specific and give details.

Does your sober living plan pay sufficient time and attention to:

	YES	I THINK SO	NO
1. A.A.	_____	_____	_____
2. Time with sponsor	_____	_____	_____
3. Spiritual Life	_____	_____	_____
4. Work	_____	_____	_____
5. Family	_____	_____	_____
6. Sleep	_____	_____	_____
7. Recreation	_____	_____	_____
8. Exercise	_____	_____	_____
9. Chores	_____	_____	_____
10. Friends	_____	_____	_____

If you have checked any of the ten items above in the "NO" or "I THINK SO" category, spend time now to strengthen that part of your plan.

Do you carry a written copy of your plan with you?

Do your spouse, sponsor and counselor each have a copy?

Have you made plans to review your progress on your sober living plan with spouse, sponsor and counselor?

Emotional Growth (Lunch)

Many recovering alcoholics who return to drinking do so by isolating themselves from people who are close to them or who know their sober living plan.

You have shared feelings, thoughts, plans and actions with other people throughout this workbook. Sharing with another person improves the chance that you will carry out your plans. Use this principle: Have at least three people involved in your sober living plan. We suggest your spouse, your A.A. sponsor and your aftercare counselor. Having these people involved does not mean that you will stay sober. This policy of sharing plans only strengthens the plan, it does not guarantee that you will carry it out.

Sharing our plans and reviewing our progress with other people has one very special feature. It keeps us out in the open. It allows us to review our feelings, thoughts and actions. It reduces the possibility of planning a drunk. If we review our sober living plan with people close to us on a regular and systematic basis and if we are honest in our review, we will lessen the possibility of planning a drunk, or having our sober living erode into a drunk. The only other possibility of a return to drinking would then be an impulse, and you have a plan to deal with impulses, don't you?

Does sharing your plans with another person threaten you? What are you feeling about sharing your plans?

How will you deal with these feelings?

Sober Life-Style (Coffee Break)

How do you plan to systematically review your sober living? If you don't have a review built in . . . DO IT! Write down when, how, where and why you will weekly review your sober living plan.

Review your plan for dealing with impulses to drink. Write out what the plan is, how you use it, when you use it.

Review your honesty plan. What is it? How do you practice it? How do you know if you are telling the truth to yourself and others?

Review your problem solving way of life. What is it? How do you practice it? How do you know when you are practicing it?

Actions for the Day (Dinner)

I   Read the Twelve Steps of A.A.

II   Practice the Twelfth Step. Do something that would count as a Twelfth Step.

III Go to an A.A. meeting. After the meeting, talk to someone about the role of the Twelfth Step and sober living.

Feelings: Review of the Day (Beverage Break)

How do you feel about finishing the workbook? Be specific. Mention all your feelings about independent sober living.

How do you think others feel about your independent sober living? Include your spouse, children, parents, employer, sponsor, and friends.

Practice feeling good about yourself. Do something to make yourself feel good.

Find time to do your relaxation exercises today.

Daily Reading (While getting ready for bed)

Pills and Ills

When you watch television, listen to the radio or read magazines, you are bombarded with advertisements for different potions and pills that offer you "instant temporary relief." Our society has become drug dependent. We have pills for headaches, stomachaches, and headaches with stomachaches. We have pills to sleep with and pills to stay awake with. If you're nervous take this, if you're tense take that. Daily, without relief, we are hammered with suggestions to use chemicals for safe, quick results. Many of these chemicals are sold over the counter without a prescription. Some are sold with a physician's prescription only. There are legitimate uses for some of these products, but most of them are physically or psychologically addicting.

The alcoholic, who is already chemically dependent, must be extremely cautious in the use of mood-altering drugs, pain relievers, tension reducers, panaceas, and pills in all sizes, shapes and colors. The idea of instant temporary relief is especially seductive to the alcoholic. The allure of this promise drew many alcoholics into the habit of alcohol abuse. Most discomforts have two direct sources. Physical discomfort is caused either by internal organ dysfunction or by external stress. Before deciding what to do about physical or psychological discomfort, assess the cause of the discomfort.

Health is that state of mind or body brought about by the efficient functioning of our physical organs and the effective interaction of ourselves with the world around us. Even if we are healthy we experience periodic discomfort. Most of the aches and pains we suffer and the ups and downs we experience will go away in time.

The body is a marvelous healer. It has the ability to take care of many of the physical discomforts we experience. Likewise, the mind is a quick, adaptive problem solver. Many problems will disappear, given enough time. The need for instant relief sends people to the pill counter before their own bodies and minds have had time to solve the problem.

Sometimes, when discomfort persists, we need to seek the attention of health professionals. When we do that, it is only prudent that we follow their advice. However, if medications are used to alter moods, emotions or consciousness, be aware that repeated use or abuse of these medications can be addicting. Talk to your physician about any medications prescribed and follow the prescription as given.

The alcoholic has to be especially wary of aches and pains. The alcoholic is accustomed to waking up sick and tired. The alcoholic used alcohol or pills to get through morning discomfort and sickness. After sobering up the alcoholic will experience discomfort like any other person. However, unlike any other person, the alcoholic has a history of chemical dependency and a habit of looking for quick, temporary relief.

The alcoholic must be especially wary of the use of any pill or chemical that in any way alters consciousness, mood or emotion. Physical or psychological discomfort, for the alcoholic, is a signal that a return to drinking is possible. When you think of using a pill, you should ask yourself, "Do I need this or do I want to alter my mood? Am I looking for reasons to avoid problem solving? Do I have a health problem?" If you have a health problem, consult a physician. Be sure to advise him that you are an alcoholic. If the physician prescribes a mood-altering drug, be sure to remind him that you have a high potential for cross-addicting to that drug. If you are unwilling to discuss this bluntly with your physician, you probably want pills for the same reason you used to want alcohol. If so, you're not far from your next drunk.

What do you do when you experience aches and pains or discomforts that incline you to reach for a pill? The first thing to do is to assess the cause of this discomfort. Is there something you can do to remove the cause of the pain? If it is a headache caused by pressure from your job what can you do?

Instead of reaching for the pill consider your other options. How can you reduce the tension and pressure of the job? Practice your problem solving skills. When experiencing discomfort and pain you may say to yourself, "Well, I'll take the pill now and solve the problem later." If you do that frequently enough you forget to solve the problem.

If aches and pains persist, or if problems can't be solved, you should seek professional advice. Be sure to inform the physician that you are an alcoholic. If you need a pill, take it only as prescribed, and be sure that the physician knows your history of chemical dependency. In general, avoid the use of chemical aids. Develop the skills necessary to relieve your own discomfort. If you need something more, see a health professional. A little discomfort now and then is better than dependency.

Reading Review

In two or three sentences, describe the point of today's reading.

How does today's reading pertain to you? Give at least two examples.

Can you implement in your life something from today's reading? Write down how you can implement today's reading in your life.

Evening Reflection (When in bed)

Think about the First Step of A.A. Review how this step relates to you. Reaffirm your commitment to Step One—"We admitted we were powerless over alcohol—that our lives had become unmanageable."

Day Twenty-Six—Keep It Simple . . .

Morning Meditation (Upon Rising)

For almost a month you have been practicing sober living through this workbook. Let's review what you've learned about yourself:

1) You're an alcoholic.
2) Drinking is the source of your alcoholism.
3) To support your drinking you told lies to yourself and to others.
4) Practicing sober living is the only way you will be healthy and free.
5) The Twelve Steps of A.A. are the means of achieving and maintaining sober living.
6) Sober living includes:
   a) telling the truth to self and others
   b) involvement in A.A.
   c) solving problems as they arise
   d) dealing with feelings
   e) work
7) You are a good person and you can be a successful sober person.

Thinking About Yourself (Breakfast)

A return to drinking is usually due to an erosion in your sober living plan. It's when things are going well and when problems are resolved, that a tendency to relax will emerge. You will want to let down. This is unwise for two reasons. First, it's when you let down on your sober living plan that you increase your chances of drinking. Second, when you let down, you will have a tendency to drift back into the old ways.

What steps have you taken to prevent yourself from letting down? Write in your notebook.

Does your plan include other people?

Who will be involved? When will they be involved? How will they help you not to let down?

Emotional Growth (Lunch)

When the child is born, it is totally self-centered. The child is entirely wrapped up with itself. Children have little ability to be concerned about anything more than their own momentary needs. Becoming a sober adult means growing beyond ourselves. It is the ability to give of ourselves to others. It is this essentially human and spiritual characteristic that lifts us into a special position in the order of the world.

Recovering alcoholics frequently have to learn to grow beyond themselves. Alcoholism is, in many ways, a singularly selfish behavior. Recovery requires breaking out of this self-imposed isolation.

Have you been selfish during your drinking career? How? Write in your notebook.

How do you feel when you think of yourself as a selfish person?

Do you have a plan or a goal to grow beyond selfishness? If so, what is the plan? If not, why not? In your plan you may want to assess how the Twelfth Step of A.A. can be of value in growing beyond selfishness.

Practice the art of giving. See yourself as an open and charitable person. Carry your sober living beyond yourself.

Sober Life-Style (Coffee Break)

How will you practice each of the Twelve Steps of A.A.? Write your answers in your notebook.

Step I—"We admitted we were powerless over alcohol—that our lives had become unmanageable." Are you an alcoholic? How are you powerless over alcohol? How had your life become unmanageable due to alcohol?

Step 2—"Came to believe that a Power greater than ourselves could restore us to sanity." Describe your belief in your Higher Power.

Step 3—"Made a decision to turn our will and our lives over to the care of God *as we understood Him*." How have you turned your life over to God?

Step 4—"Made a searching and fearless moral inventory

of ourselves." Did you take a moral inventory? Was it as thorough as you could make it?

Step 5—"Admitted to God, to ourselves, and to another human being the exact nature of our wrongs." Did you admit your wrongs to God? Did you admit your wrongs to yourself? Did you admit your wrongs to another human being?

Step 6—"Were entirely ready to have God remove all these defects of character." How did you ready yourself to have God remove your defects of character?

Step 7—"Humbly asked Him to remove all our short-comings." Did you do this? Review the way you did this.

Step 8—"Made a list of all persons we had harmed, and became willing to make amends to them all." Did you make a list? Did you check it? Are you willing to make amends to all persons you have harmed?

Step 9—"Made direct amends to such people wherever possible, except when to do so would injure them or others." Did you do this? Explain who, what, when, and where.

Step 10—"Continued to take personal inventory and when we were wrong promptly admitted it." What is your schedule for taking the Tenth Step? Do you think you will take a Tenth Step regularly?

Step 11—"Sought through prayer and meditation to improve our conscious contact with God *as we understood Him,* praying only for knowledge of His will for us and the power to carry that out." Do you pray and meditate daily? Do you have a special time each day put aside for prayer and meditation? Are you prepared to accept God's will for you?

Step 12—"Having had a spiritual awakening as the result of these steps, we tried to carry this message to alcoholics, and to practice these principles in all our affairs." What is your Twelfth Step plan?

Actions for the Day (Dinner)

I   Go to an A.A. meeting.

II   Help clean up after the meeting.

III   Find someone to whom you can give of yourself. Remember, your time and attention is often the best gift you have to offer.

Feelings: Review of the Day (Beverage Break)

Practice feeling:

a) good about yourself
b) relaxed
c) a sense of accomplishment

Find a quiet place to work on these emotions.

Daily Reading (While getting ready for bed)

Developing The Habit Of Reading

For nearly a month you have been working daily on this workbook. This activity includes a daily reading assignment. This daily reading enhances your sober living. It is a good habit to maintain.

You probably are looking forward to finishing this workbook, not only as a milepost on your personal road to recovery and sober living, but also because the workbook is time-consuming. However, you would not have come this far if you did not feel the time was well spent. We suggest that you continue this daily habit. Read something every day that will reinforce your sober living.

What should you read? There are many A.A. books, such as the *Big Book* or *Twenty-Four Hours A Day*. These are good for a start. You may also want to visit a public library. If you agree that this personal reading time can be beneficial to you, then you could map out a reading plan. If you decide to visit a public library, look in the area of self-help books and personal problem solving books. Do not overlook the biography and autobiography sections. There is tremendous value in reading about the life of another person.

Develop a personal reading plan. Don't just promise yourself you will do it. Instead, find the time to go to the library. Get a book and begin to spend a minimum of fifteen minutes per day reading something which will aid you in your sober living.

Reading Review

In two or three sentences, describe the point of today's reading.

How does today's reading pertain to you? Give at least two examples.

Can you implement in your life something from today's reading? Write down how you can implement today's reading in your life.

Evening Reflection (When in bed)

Think of a holy person you like, such as Christ, Buddha, Mohammed, or Moses. Think about how that holy person rose above personal selfishness. Contemplate the implications of imitating that holy person's style of charity.

Day Twenty-Seven—*Easy Does It . . .*

Morning Meditation (Upon Rising)

This is the next-to-last day for working in the sober living workbook. This thought should arouse both a sense of relief and a sense of anxiety.

Yesterday we spoke of sliding into a drunk because things were going so well that you stopped paying attention to everything that was keeping you sober.

Today we want to focus on a return to drinking because of an increase in problems as the result of sober living. This does not necessarily mean that new problems emerge, but perhaps now, for the first time, you are beginning to see all the problems in your life which your drinking created or intensified. For example, perhaps debts which had piled up while you were drinking are coming due now.

What new problems have emerged since you've been sober?

Thinking About Yourself (Breakfast)

Are there latent problems in your life that might cause you future difficulty? Write in your notebook.

There are two ways you can approach these potential problems. The first is to ignore them and hope they either go away or do not emerge. The second is to deal with these potential problems in a problem solving manner.

You can take each problem and approach it as if it is real or as if it someday will be real. The next thing to do is to approach it in a problem solving manner. Choose one of the latent problems that could interfere with your sober living in the future.

1) What is the exact nature of the problem? Be as precise as possible, even though the problem is still in the future. Write in your notebook.

2) How would you like to solve the problem? What would your goals be?

3) Develop a plan to solve the problem. Be specific and precise.

4) Implement the plan when the problem emerges.

5) Review your progress on problem solution in a systematic fashion.

You cannot anticipate all problems, but your strategy of personal problem solving will allow you to soberly and maturely deal with your problems as they emerge.

Emotional Growth (Lunch)

Make a list of emotions you feel comfortable handling. For example, emotions like love, friendship, envy, loneliness, or depression. Write down the emotions you feel comfortable experiencing and expressing.

Describe how you deal with each of the emotions you listed. When have you experienced each one? What feelings are you left with after you experience and express each of these emotions?

Make a list of emotions you still have difficulty experiencing and expressing. For example, emotions like resentment, anger or love.

Now, for each of these emotions, describe how you intend to develop your skills for dealing with them. Be specific. In other words, what is your plan for emotional growth in the three emotions listed above?

Sober Life-Style (Coffee Break)

Write a paragraph or two entitled, *My Sober Life-Style*. Don't be afraid to express yourself. Be as specific and as detailed as possible. Writing down a description of your sober life-style will help you conceptualize your life-style and carry out that life-style.

Actions for the Day (Dinner)

I   Go to an A.A. meeting.

II   Practice the Twelfth Step.

III   Call up a friend and make arrangements to meet. Use this time just to enjoy one another's company. Friendship is one of the most important attributes of sober living.

Feelings: Review of the Day (Beverage Break)

I   How does it feel to be on the next-to-last day of the workbook? Write in your notebook.

II   Why not share this feeling with another person? What is your reaction to the idea of sharing your feelings?

III Practice relaxation exercises.
     Practice feeling good.
     Practice feeling accomplished.

Daily Reading (While getting ready for bed)

A Sense of Accomplishment

In A.A. you frequently hear, "Easy Does It" and "One Day at a Time." These two sayings have a lot of meaning for the recovering alcoholic. Sober living is a mature life-style built upon daily decision-making. However, in this systematic, regular and routine approach to life, an individual sometimes does not achieve a sense of accomplishment.

Take time out. Periodically review what you have been doing. Look at your life. Don't be especially critical, rather let the good things you've been accomplishing flow into your attention. Many recovering alcoholics focus on their mistakes. There is value in keeping an eye on what drinking did to you, but periodically allow yourself a sense of accomplishment.

"Let the sunshine in" is a line from a once-popular song. It can also be a theme song for the recovering alcoholic. Let the sunshine in. See what is good about yourself. Learn to rejoice in the good that you have. Take time out and make an inventory of everything you have going for yourself. You may be shocked. We know many of the negative things about ourselves, but rarely do we take stock of what is positive.

There is a man who completed his sober living workbook several years ago and has been practicing sober living ever since. He was recently asked what had been the most important part of his recovery. He answered, "Learning to appreciate what I had going for me." He added that he makes every Thursday his personal-sense-of-accomplishment day. Every

Thursday he reviews what he has accomplished. He looks at the good things in his life and is grateful for them.

Why don't you pick a day to strengthen your sense of accomplishment?

Reading Review

In two or three sentences, describe the point of today's reading.

How does today's reading pertain to you? Give at least two examples.

Can you implement in your life something from today's reading? Write down how you can implement today's reading in your life.

Evening Reflection (When in bed)

During this evening's reflection, dwell on all the good things in your life. Think about all that you have going for yourself. Feel a sense of accomplishment. Let the sunshine in.

Day Twenty-Eight—*Live and Let Live . . .*

Morning Meditation (Upon Rising)

Think about a warm spring morning. Regardless of the time of year or the weather think about a warm spring morning. Let your heart and soul feel alive and new and ready to begin again.

Spend some time reviewing all you have accomplished over the past four weeks. Think of what brought you to the point of needing this workbook. After a few moments of recollection, think of what you have learned these past four weeks. Focus on what this experience means to you. During the last part of this morning's meditation, think about your future. How do you want to live your life? Picture yourself as a sober, mature, responsible person.

This is the last time that you will have this workbook for morning meditation. It is a good sober living habit to spend a few minutes each morning in spiritual awakening. You have begun this habit. You may want to think seriously about the role of a morning meditation and implement it in your life.

Thinking About Yourself (Breakfast)

You have learned many things. You have made plans to live soberly. It is up to you to fulfill your plans. Start with a happy heart and a good feeling. You will practice sober living and will be happy doing it. Please review the following items.

I   You are an alcoholic. You are powerless over alcohol and your life becomes unmanageable due to alcohol.

II   You have become an active member of Alcoholics Anonymous. Your practice of the Twelve Steps and Traditions of A.A. and your involvement with your sponsor and home group will maintain sobriety.

III You have developed a sober living plan and shared it with your spouse, sponsor, employer and aftercare counselor. Daily practice of the sober living plan will lead to a happy and successful life.

IV You are in touch with the truth and with telling the truth to yourself and others at all times. You are in touch with your feelings and express them in healthy ways. You know how to identify impulses to drink and how to handle impulses to drink. You have a philosophy of problem solving. You have examined your wrongdoings and confessed them to God and another person. You have an aftercare plan that will help you to weekly review all that you have learned.

V   Start in peace. Practice sober living every day.

What are your thoughts on your last day of this workbook? Write in your notebook.

What doubts do you still have about yourself?

What are your plans for dealing with your doubts?

Practice thinking of yourself as a winner. See yourself alive, sober, involved in A.A. and happy. Maximize your assets. Be a winner.

Emotional Growth (Lunch)

Part of your recovery from alcoholism has rested on your ability to recognize your feelings and express them in a healthy, happy and sober fashion.

How do you feel about yourself now, as opposed to when you first started the workbook and your recovery program? Write in your notebook.

Have you shared your feelings about this day and about yourself with another person? If not, do so. If so, what was the other person's response to your feelings?

Sober Life-Style (Coffee Break)

The Twelve Steps of Alcoholics Anonymous are listed below. These steps have guided you toward sober living. The continued and regular practice of these steps will keep you sober. Read each step. Think about each step. Renew in your heart your acceptance and commitment to each step.

1. "We admitted we were powerless over alcohol—that our lives had become unmanageable."

2. "Came to believe that a Power greater than ourselves could restore us to sanity."

3. "Made a decision to turn our will and our lives over to the care of God *as we understood Him.*"

4. "Made a searching and fearless moral inventory of ourselves."

5. "Admitted to God, to ourselves, and to another human being the exact nature of our wrongs."

6. "Were entirely ready to have God remove all these defects of character."

7. "Humbly asked Him to remove our shortcomings."

8. "Made a list of all persons we had harmed, and became willing to make amends to them all."

9. "Made direct amends to such people wherever possible, except when to do so would injure them or others."

10. "Continue to take personal inventory and when we were wrong promptly admitted it."

11. "Sought through prayer and meditation to improve our conscious contact with God *as we understoo Him,* praying only for knowledge of His will for us an the power to carry that out."

12. "Having had a spiritual awakening as the result of these steps, we tried to carry this message to alcoholics, and to practice these principles in all our affairs."

Actions for the Day (Dinner)

I   Review your sober living schedule one last time. Is it as well-balanced as you want it to be? Is there sufficient time devoted to the essential areas of life? Practice honesty. Review in your head each of the ten essential life areas. Is your life as well-balanced as you can make it? Don't rush through this exercise even though you have done it twice before. Your sober living plan is your life. It's the way you intend to live. Will you get regular sleep, get the chores done when they need to be done, and recreate as scheduled? Take the time now to review each essential area. Think of the importance of each area. Fill in the following chart for each essential life area. Is your schedule well-balanced?

	YES	MAYBE	NO
Work	_____	_____	_____
Sleep	_____	_____	_____
Food	_____	_____	_____
Exercise	_____	_____	_____
A.A.	_____	_____	_____
Recreation	_____	_____	_____
Spiritual Development	_____	_____	_____
Family Activities	_____	_____	_____
Friends	_____	_____	_____
Chores	_____	_____	_____

Any item you checked "maybe" or "no" needs to be reviewed. Sober living is well-balanced living. It is the happy mixture of activities you must do with activities you want to do. (Assuming that what you want to do is healthy for you.) The sober living plan should be your guide for the next year. Take the time now to fill out a sober living plan. Make sure all of the essentials of sober living are listed. If you make changes in the plan, telephone the people (spouse, A.A. sponsor, employer, counselor) with whom you have shared your original plan. Explain why you changed the plan. Try not to be defensive. If good ideas emerge from these telephone calls, incorporate them into your sober living plan.

II Go to an A.A. meeting. Tell your A.A. friends that you have completed the workbook. Tell those who have time to listen about your sober living plan and how you intend to carry it out.

III Implement your sober living plan and stick to it for at least one year.

Sober Living Schedule

	MORNING	AFTERNOON	EVENING NIGHT
Friday			
Thursday			
Wednesday			
Tuesday			
Monday			
Sunday			
Saturday			

6:00 a.m.
7:00 a.m.
8:00 a.m.
9:00 a.m.
10:00 a.m.
11:00 a.m.
12:00 p.m.
1:00 p.m.
2:00 p.m.
3:00 p.m.
4:00 p.m.
5:00 p.m.
6:00 p.m.
7:00 p.m.
8:00 p.m.
9:00 p.m.
10:00 p.m.
11:00 p.m.
12:00 a.m.
1:00 a.m.
2:00 a.m.
3:00 a.m.
4:00 a.m.
5:00 a.m.

Feelings: Review of the Day (Beverage Break)

Emotional expression and development are areas of special need for the recovering alcoholic. The chemical ethyl alcohol has hindered your emotional development and expression. Since becoming sober, you have worked at identifying emotions, labeling them and channeling emotional energy into constructive outlets.

You have completed exercises designed to teach you to feel good about yourself, relax under stress, and feel good about your accomplishments. These exercises should be practiced regularly. Develop the habit of practicing one exercise each night while lying in bed before falling asleep. Practice feeling good, feeling relaxed and feeling accomplished.

Daily Reading (While getting ready for bed)

The End

You see the words "The End" at the close of every movie. They usually signify that the story is over. However, in your situation, the end is just a beginning. You have accomplished four weeks of sober living. You have taken time to assess your strengths and weaknesses. You have put your house in order. But, and this is a *big* but, this is not the end of what you learned. It is only the beginning of putting into practice all that you have learned.

Many people falter at this point. They found daily treatment a challenge even though it was hard work. They had a sense of challenge, a mountain to climb. Well, you have accomplished this, but unlike the mountain climber, you cannot descend to the old ways. For you there can be no return to the old ways. Yet you cannot maintain the intensity and zeal, the drive and energy you put into the last four weeks. What do you do? First of all you recognize your accomplishments for what they are. Praise yourself. Give yourself applause and then push on to new goals.

Many recovering alcoholics are hard on themselves. They find it difficult to praise themselves. They fail to see their accomplishments and they tend to focus on their failures. This is your opportunity to avoid that. Sit down and review what brought you to this point. Look at what you did, the price you paid to change your ways. Now give yourself credit for solving the problem. Many alcoholics never do anything about their problems. They find all the reasons in the world to assure themselves that they cannot change, or that they do not want to change. But you did something about your problem and that in itself is commendable.

Beware of one more trap, the pitfall of over-elation or over-confidence. Many recovering alcoholics become over-confident and, almost without thinking, resort to old ways and reward themselves with a drink. Perhaps the best way to reward yourself for achieving sober living is with a party. At this get-together, invite people who will be especially happy to see you doing well. Treat it like a small birthday party.

Involving others in your sober living accomplishments is the best way to insure continued success. If you keep your successes a secret you may think that others remember only the drinking you. If you tell those you trust about your recovery you may receive love, attention and praise for doing well, and your sober living practices will be out in the open. The more you keep your successes in the open, the more you will succeed.

Finally, you should take this opportunity to set new goals. The recovering alcoholic needs goals. Without goals you take the risk of becoming bored and slipping back to the old ways. What kind of goals should you set? Goals you can reach. Always stack the deck in your favor. Set goals you can reach. Be a winner.

Live in peace. Practice sober living every day and your life can be what you make it.

Evening Reflection (When in bed)

Feel inner peace and love for yourself. You are a good person. You have taken a great step toward sober living. Feel good about it.

Be grateful. Thank God, yourself, and the people who have helped you during this initial period of recovery. Feel gratitude. Think about ways to express your gratitude to all of them.

Close this book contemplating inner peace. Strive for peace within yourself. Picture yourself an as instrument of peace.